CONTENTS

Introduction V

Lesson 1: **God Saves People** 1

Lesson 2: **God Gathers People** 15

Lesson 3: **God Scatters People** 29

Lesson 4: **God Sends People** 45

Lesson 5: **God Connects People** 61

Lesson 6: **God Gifts People** 77

Leader's Guide 91

About the Authors 95

The Jesus Bible

STUDY SERIES

CHURCH

THE STORY OF JESUS ON DISPLAY TO THE WORLD

Aaron Coe, Ph.D.

Series Writer & General Editor of The Jesus Bible

Matt Rogers, Ph.D.

Series Writer & Lead Writer of The Jesus Bible

 Harper*Christian* Resources

 passionpublishing

The Jesus Bible Study Series: Church
© 2024 by Passion Publishing

Requests for information should be addressed to:
HarperChristian Resources, 3900 Sparks Dr. SE, Grand Rapids, Michigan 49546

ISBN 978-0-310-15506-5 (softcover)
ISBN 978-0-310-15507-2 (ebook)

HarperChristian Resources titles may be purchased in bulk for church, business, fundraising, or ministry use. For information, please e-mail ResourceSpecialist@ChurchSource.com.

First printing March 2024 / Printed in the United States of America

INTRODUCTION

Jesus is the hero of the Bible. This may sound like an overly simple statement to make, but this truth helps us to make sense out of the sixty-six books of the Bible that can often seem intimidating. There is no doubt that the Bible is a daunting collection of texts, filled with complex concepts and intricate stories. It's easy for any reader to get lost and miss the main point of God's story. Jesus is the point.

As a reminder, this is the fifth of six "acts" in God's beautiful overarching story told throughout Scripture: (1) *Beginnings*, (2) *Revolt*, (3) *People*, (4) *Savior*, (5) *Church*, (6) *Forever*. Throughout this series, we have seen how Jesus was present in each of these main movements. He was there at the beginning, creating all things and fashioning a world that was meant to bring him glory (see John 1:1–4). He was there when the first humans, unwilling to live under God's rule, staged a revolt and pursued their own ways. The consequence of their actions was death, yet God promised a child would be born who would crush Satan's head and rescue humanity from the punishment of sin (see Genesis 3:15). This promised Savior of the people would not arrive until the New Testament, but hints of his coming were seen in prophecies foretold throughout the Old Testament (see, for example, Isaiah 53:1–12).

Jesus is the *Savior*. His story is one of perfect obedience to the Father. He lived a sinless life and succeeded where everyone else failed (see Hebrews 4:15). Then, in a stunning act, he paid the ultimate price for sin by offering his own life as a sacrifice (see 1 Peter 2:23). His victorious resurrection proved that he had accomplished what he had set out to do (see Romans 5:12–19). The disciple Peter declared of him: "Salvation is found in no one else, for there is no other name under heaven given to mankind by which we must be saved" (Acts 4:12).

Throughout this study, we will explore how the early followers of Jesus, after his ascension into heaven (see Acts 1:9), came together to form what we call the *church.* We will see that God intended the church to be the body of Christ—bone of his bone and flesh of his flesh (see Ephesians 1:22–23)—and serve to bring people into his kingdom. The church is the method God uses to gather his people together, connect them in fellowship with one another, gift his people, and then send them back out into the world to spread the message of salvation.

Of course, we all have different associations today with "the church." For some, church is just a place we have visited in the past or observed from a distance. For others among us, the church brings up not-so-pleasant memories and not-so-great feelings because of certain people or attitudes we have encountered there. But fortunately, there are also those among us who have had the glorious privilege of experiencing life in a healthy church. We understand the joy that can come from worshiping Jesus together with God's people.

Whatever your thoughts and feelings are about the church . . . *welcome*. We are glad that you have made the decision to step into this study. We pray that God uses this study to shape your love for his people and the community of believers that is his church. As Paul writes, "His intent was that now, through the church, the manifold wisdom of God should be made known" (Ephesians 3:10). Simply put, the church is the way that you (and others) can see and experience the wisdom of God. How cool is that! God has big plans for his church, and we pray that these plans will be seen and realized in your life today.

—Aaron & Matt

Lesson One

GOD SAVES PEOPLE

The LORD had said to Abram, "Go from your country, your people and your father's household to the land I will show you. I will make you into a great nation, and I will bless you; I will make your name great, and you will be a blessing."

GENESIS 12:1–2

Consequently, you are no longer foreigners and strangers, but fellow citizens with God's people and also members of his household, built on the foundation of the apostles and prophets, with Christ Jesus himself as the chief cornerstone.

EPHESIANS 2:19–22

Everyone who
calls on the
name of the Lord
will be saved.

ACTS 2:21

WELCOME

Certain words evoke images in our mind. When we hear those words, we immediately associate them with people and places. Sometimes, these words conjure up fond memories. Other times, the emotions that are stirred up are ones we would like to forget.

Recently, I (Aaron) and my wife, Carmen, celebrated our twenty-fifth wedding anniversary by taking a trip to the beach for a week. We had a wonderful time, and there are images from that trip that are now locked into my mind. In particular, I remember details such as the hotel where we were staying lighting three torches on the edge of their pool to mark the sunset each evening. Now, whenever I see a flaming torch, I am reminded of that trip.

You may have similar memories of a place you visited or an experience you went through that are now etched into your mind because of your positive associations with it. But it's also likely that you have endured experiences in your past that have left you with not-so-positive memories. Perhaps, for example, you can remember a song that was popular when you went through a breakup. Now, every time you hear that song—even though it may be years or even decades later—it brings you back to that difficult time in your life.

As we touched on in the introduction, our past experiences with the church can bring up these same kinds of emotions in us—both positive and negative. We may view the church as a whole either positively or negatively, based on what we witnessed certain people doing in the churches where we grew up or attended in the past. If the people were kindhearted, generous, and engaged in serving others, we likely have positive associations. On the other hand, if we experienced people being mean-spirited, stingy, and engaged in putting down others, we may have negative associations. The church is made up of people, and as we all know only too well, people have just as much capability of being accepting and loving as they do of being judgmental and spiteful.

So, our past experiences with a congregation—good and bad—will often shape our current perceptions. But here is the interesting thing about the church: *it's not what we think about it that matters.* When we dig into the pages of the New Testament, as we will be doing in this study, what we find is that the church is not an institution formed according to the whims of people but an entity divinely ordained by God from the start.

Now, this does not negate what we have experienced with churches in the past. It certainly doesn't dismiss the reality that the church is made up of fallen human beings and, as a result, evil will creep into God's sacred assembly from time to time. But it should change our perceptions as to the overall purpose and mission of the church. Regardless of our experiences with a local church, God has a purpose and mission for the body of Christ as a whole. This is where we will begin—by looking at God's purpose for the church as it relates to saving people.

1. What personal experiences have influenced your perception of the church?

2. How would you describe what the church is and what its mission is to the world?

READ

A Place Where Relationships Are Restored

The apostle Paul describes the plight of humanity as follows: "As for you, you were dead in your transgressions and sins, in which you used to live when you followed the ways of this world" (Ephesians 2:1–2). Paul states that we were spiritually dead because of sin—we were enemies of God and subject to his wrath. But then, "God, who is rich in mercy, made us alive with Christ" (verses 4–5). We have been brought back into a right relationship with God because of Jesus' work. This is the "vertical dimension" of our salvation. We are made one with God.

However, sin does more than just disrupt our relationship with God. Paul goes on to describe another aspect to our salvation that we might call the "horizontal dimension." When we come to salvation, we are not only made right with God (vertical) but are also brought into right relationship with each another (horizontal). Paul uses the image of a dividing wall to show how God, though Christ, breaks down the kinds of division that sin creates:

> ¹¹ *Therefore, remember that formerly you who are Gentiles by birth and called "uncircumcised" by those who call themselves "the circumcision" (which is done in the body by human hands)—* ¹² *remember that at that time you were separate from Christ, excluded from citizenship in Israel and foreigners to the covenants of the promise, without hope and without God in the world.* ¹³ *But now in Christ Jesus you who once were far away have been brought near by the blood of Christ.*
>
> ¹⁴ *For he himself is our peace, who has made the two groups one and has destroyed the barrier, the dividing wall of hostility,* ¹⁵ *by setting aside in his flesh the law with its commands and regulations. His purpose was to create in himself one new humanity out of the two, thus making peace,* ¹⁶ *and in one body to reconcile both of them to God through the cross, by which he put to death their hostility.* ¹⁷ *He came and preached peace to you who were far away and peace to those who were near.* ¹⁸ *For through him we both have access to the Father by one Spirit.*
>
> Ephesians 2:11–18

Paul is making a stunning argument in this passage. It's not just that the work of Jesus unites *certain* people together. Rather, the work of Jesus unites *all* people together. In Paul's day, a great divide existed between two people groups—the Jews and the Gentiles. As Paul states, the Gentiles were "excluded from citizenship in Israel and foreigners to the covenants of the promise" (verse 12). They were on the outside. But now, these Gentiles "who once were far away have been brought near by the blood of Christ" (verse 13).

In our day, we don't tend to think in terms of Jews and Gentiles. But these two groups are the core of the Bible's story. Back in Genesis 12:1–2, God told Abram (later renamed Abraham) that he would become the father of a great nation. Later, through his family, the nation of Israel (the Jews) came into being. This group of people were at the center of God's work, particularly in the Old Testament. They received God's miraculous freedom from slavery in Egypt. They were given God's law. God instituted the priesthood and sacrificial system through Israel. They even inherited a great land on which the nation would exist. God promised that the Savior—his answer to sin and death—would come from this nation.

But God's salvation was never meant for Israel alone. In fact, God told Abram that his people would live as a blessing to the other nations. Israel was meant to showcase the Lord's work among a set group of people so that all nations would see and know the one true God.

3. Why do you think God wants us to not only have a right "vertical" relationship with him but also right "horizontal" relationships with others?

4. What are some of the divisions that you see among Christians today? What does Ephesians 2:11–18 say about God's intent to break down these divisions?

A Unifying Force

Throughout the Old Testament, the nation of Israel—even though they had been chosen as a special covenant people—repeatedly fell short of the divine purposes that God envisioned for them. The Lord had provided them with clear guidance in life and established laws to lead them in righteousness, but they continually deviated from his intended path. As depicted in the book of Judges, the Israelites would turn away from God, engage in idol worship, face the consequences of their disobedience through oppression by foreign nations, and then repent, prompting God to raise up judges for their deliverance. This recurring cycle highlighted the ongoing struggle of the people to align with the moral and spiritual standards set by God.

The prophetic books—including Isaiah, Jeremiah, and Ezekiel—echoed God's lamentation over Israel's failure to fulfill his intended purposes. The prophets condemned the people for their social injustice, corruption, and neglect of the marginalized. Despite God's desire for them to be a beacon of light to the nations, they succumbed to worldly temptations and neglected their responsibility to live in accordance with God's moral and ethical standards. The Old Testament presents a nuanced portrayal of the relationship between God and Israel—one marked by divine disappointment in the face of the nation's consistent disobedience and their inability to fully embody the intended purposes outlined in the covenant.

However, just because the people did not always get it right doesn't mean that God gave up on them . . . or the other nations. He sent Jesus to pay the price for sin—both for the Jews and for all the other nation groups (the Gentiles). Paul goes on to write:

> [19] *Consequently, you are no longer foreigners and strangers, but fellow citizens with God's people and also members of his household,* [20] *built on the*

foundation of the apostles and prophets, with Christ Jesus himself as the chief cornerstone. [21] In him the whole building is joined together and rises to become a holy temple in the Lord. [22] And in him you too are being built together to become a dwelling in which God lives by his Spirit.

Ephesians 2:19–22

Jesus brings everything together. All those who receive him by faith (see verse 8) become one with God and with each other. They are made a part of God's church, which is simply another way of saying that everyone who is saved by Jesus is made a part of his people.

Paul underscores that God, by placing everything under the authority of Jesus and appointing him as the head over the church, is orchestrating a unifying force that surpasses cultural, ethnic, and national distinctions. This divine arrangement emphasizes the inclusive nature of Jesus' mission, signaling that his redemptive work is designed to unite individuals from diverse corners of the world. The church, described as the body of Christ, serves as the tangible manifestation of this unity, with believers, regardless of their backgrounds, invited to partake in the fullness of Christ, who fills every aspect of existence.

The understanding of the church as the body of Christ solidifies the concept that Jesus brings all nations together. As individuals are incorporated into the body of Christ through faith, they become integral components of a larger, interconnected whole. This metaphor underscores the unity, diversity, and shared purpose of believers globally. Essentially, Jesus' redemptive work not only reconciles individuals with God but also cultivates a global community, dismantling the barriers that once separated humanity and establishing a harmonious fellowship of diverse believers under the leadership of Christ.

5. What did God want the Israelites to portray about himself and his nature to the nations around them? How successful were they in this mission to the world?

6. What does God want the church to portray about the kinds of people he accepts into his family? How successful has the church been in revealing this to the world?

A Building and a Body

Notice in Ephesians 2:19–22 that Paul depicts the church as a building, with Jesus being the cornerstone. Christ is the most important part of the structure. Without him, there would be no church. The apostles and prophets comprise the foundation—these were the men and women who were a part of God's work throughout the Bible and whom the Spirit of God used to reveal his Word. Then come all the other people. They were once strangers and aliens, separated from God and from one another. Now they are citizens, saints, and members of God's house.

Peter uses the same image to describe the church when he writes, "You also, like living stones, are being built into a spiritual house . . . offering spiritual sacrifices acceptable to God through Jesus Christ" (1 Peter 2:5). Peter portrays God as a great builder who takes "living stones" and places them in his church, where they will worship God and offer spiritual sacrifices because of Jesus. It's not that the church is a building—though the church may well worship in a building—but that the church is people who have been saved by grace and are placed together into a building that God has been constructing since the beginning of the world.

The image of a building isn't the only way that Paul helps us understand the role of the church. In the following passage, he likens the church to a human body:

> *[11] So Christ himself gave the apostles, the prophets, the evangelists, the pastors and teachers, [12] to equip his people for works of service, so that the body*

of Christ may be built up [13] *until we all reach unity in the faith and in the knowledge of the Son of God and become mature, attaining to the whole measure of the fullness of Christ.*

[14] *Then we will no longer be infants, tossed back and forth by the waves, and blown here and there by every wind of teaching and by the cunning and craftiness of people in their deceitful scheming.* [15] *Instead, speaking the truth in love, we will grow to become in every respect the mature body of him who is the head, that is, Christ.* [16] *From him the whole body, joined and held together by every supporting ligament, grows and builds itself up in love, as each part does its work.*

Ephesians 4:11–16

The church is like a body, with Jesus as the head (see also Colossians 1:18). Of course, without a head the body can't function, just like without a cornerstone a building is worthless. When people enter into the church through salvation, they are made a part of God's body. They are living, active parts of that body—growing into the full stature of manhood or womanhood. The goal, just like the actual development of the human body, is maturity.

God takes those he saves and fits them together in his body. As Paul writes, "Just as a body, though one, has many parts, but all its many parts form one body, so it is with Christ" (1 Corinthians 12:12). This reality helps us see that there is really only one church, comprised of all those who know and love Jesus. This massive group of humanity, both Jew and Gentile alike, are a part of God's body, the church. Those in the church, then, are called to unity because they are—quite literally—a part of the same body. Disunity and infighting among Christians is an affront to the unity that God purchased for them through the sacrifice of Jesus Christ.

God's Spirit equips his people with varying gifts to help them serve as a meaningful part of the whole. Paul expands on this picture when he writes, "For just as each of us has one body with many members, and these members do not all have the same function, so in Christ we, though many, form one body, and each member belongs to all the others" (Romans 12:4–5). Not every part of the body has the same function, but they are all necessary. No one should disparage the gifts of others or minimize their own place in the body. All people are necessary.

7. How does the image of the church as a building, with Christ as the cornerstone, help you to understand how God wants his people to function within it?

8. How does the image of the church as a body, with Christ as the head, help you to understand how God wants every person to contribute in it?

REFLECT

There is one final picture in Ephesians that can help us make sense of the church. Paul writes, "'For this reason a man will leave his father and mother and be united to his wife, and the two will become one flesh.' This is a profound mystery—but I am talking about Christ and the church. However, each one of you also must love his wife as he loves himself, and the wife must respect her husband" (Ephesians 5:31–33).

Paul depicts the church as a bride and Jesus as the bridegroom. Christ's model of sacrificial love is indicative of the posture of husbands who love their wives and give of themselves for their spouses' highest good. Paul even says that God created marriage as a way of putting this type of love on display. God had a plan for marriage, and it was more than just companionship or earthly happiness. He wanted to show the world how he loves his church and how his church should respond to that love.

It is stunning to consider that God would choose to be joined to the church. In our day, it's common for a smitten husband to say that he "married up," meaning that his wife was way out of his league. The opposite is true of God. He did not marry up.

He bound himself to the church in love, even though he knew she would prove adulterous time and time again. This is the point made in the Old Testament book of Hosea, where God is pictured as a husband who pursues and marries a prostitute. He continually takes her back, even though she repeatedly proves wayward. God says this is the way that he loves his church.

God doesn't love his church with mere sentimentality or affection. His love is active. It's costly. Paul uses five descriptions in Ephesians 5:25–27 to describe Jesus' actions toward her: (1) He loved the church (verse 25), (2) he gave himself up for the church (verse 25), (3) he purified the church (verse 26), (4) he cleansed the church (verse 26), and (5) he will present the church to himself (verse 27). These descriptions call to mind a wedding day when the bride prepares herself for her husband. If you've ever watched a bride's face as she walked down the aisle, then you have a sense of Jesus' love for the church. The church should worship, adore, and serve Jesus with this same kind of singular and overwhelming love.

9. What do Paul's words in Ephesians 5:25–32 reveal about God's love for his church? What are some ways that you have experienced this love?

10. How does the way Jesus sees the church—as a bride—compare to the way you see the church? What would change if you saw the church as Jesus does?

CLOSE

What was God's intent in establishing the church? As Paul writes, the Lord created the church so that his wisdom "should be made known to the rulers and authorities in the heavenly realms" (Ephesians 3:10). The church is the vehicle through which he reveals his plan throughout the entire world. In the church, we see sinners who have been saved by God's grace worshiping the one who saved them. The church makes God's salvation visible to the world. It proves that God can and does save anyone and everyone who comes to him. The rulers and authorities in the heavenly places look down on the church in awe of God's plan.

It is clear, then, that the church wasn't formed by accident. The church was God's plan from the very foundation of the world. Even better, God has promised to protect his church forever and protect those in his church from the evil one (see John 17:15). The church of Jesus Christ will last until the time when Jesus returns and makes all things new. Until then, God will continue to save sinners, place them as living stones in his spiritual house, fashion them to play a meaningful role in his body, and purify them as a radiant bride.

11. What do you think would need to happen in order for the church as a whole to more accurately reflect its intended design?

12. What role does the church play in your life at present? When you tell other people about your church, what do you tell them that makes it special?

Lesson Two

GOD GATHERS PEOPLE

*"Then the L*ORD* your God will restore your fortunes and have compassion on you and gather you again from all the nations where he scattered you."*

DEUTERONOMY 30:3

From him the whole body, joined and held together by every supporting ligament, grows and builds itself up in love, as each part does its work.

EPHESIANS 4:16

But if we walk in

the light . . .

we have fellowship

with one another.

1 JOHN 1:7

WELCOME

Life is made up of "we and me" scenarios. When you get a new job, you become a part of a larger team. That team has collective responsibilities and goals, and those objectives cannot be accomplished without the collective "we." However, the "me" part is the role that you, the individual, play in the organization. You are bringing your unique gifts and talents to the table. In a sense, the organization would not be the same without you.

When I was just out of high school, I got a job building homes. In the homebuilding process, there was one goal that "we" all had: to build a house that people could enjoy. However, to accomplish this overall goal, there were dozens of "me" specialties that individuals or individual teams performed. Painters, electricians, framers, and landscapers were all crucial to the success of each project. Homebuilding is very much a "we and me" endeavor.

The church is an example of "we and me." It is common to hear a person say, "Jesus died for me." This is a truth that is vital to understanding the Christian faith. We are all born sinners who, because of our sin, are separated from God. Jesus lived a perfect life, died for our sin, and rose victorious over Satan, sin, and death. By faith, we can trust in Jesus' work and receive God's salvation. When we do, we are given the "right to become children of God" (John 1:12). This is an individual decision and a personal privilege. We become Christians as individuals—not based on the faith of anyone else. Faith is not a group decision.

However, Jesus didn't merely die for the "me" but for the "we." When we think of our personal faith in Jesus, we can lose sight of the fact that God not only saves people individually but also saves them to a community. When we trust in Jesus for salvation, we become part of a larger body of believers called the church. As we discussed in the previous lesson, this church is comprised of all people, across all centuries, who have put their faith in Christ. It is made up of people from varying races, socioeconomic backgrounds, political affiliations, and genders. It is vast, it is beautiful, and it is God's plan for putting his saving wisdom on display (see Ephesians 3:10). Our individual salvation isn't really individual after all.

1. What happens if you live as if salvation is only about you?

2. What power does the church possess when it embraces its collective "we"?

READ

A Promise to Regather

In various instances throughout the Old Testament, the people of Israel faced consequences for their disobedience to God's commandments. The scattering of the Israelites among different nations was a result of their turning away from God and embracing idolatry and sinful practices. This scattering served as a form of discipline and correction, illustrating the importance of obedience in maintaining a close relationship with God. We see examples of this in the Assyrian captivity, when the kingdom of Israel was taken into exile (see 2 Kings 17:23), and the Babylonian captivity, when the kingdom of Judah was taken into exile (see Jeremiah 29:10).

In the midst of the hardships of captivity and dispersion, God consistently offered hope to his people through promises of restoration. The Lord, in his mercy and compassion, had told his people before they even entered into the Promised Land that he would gather them from the places where they would be scattered. This gathering would represent not only a physical return to their land but also a spiritual restoration and reconciliation with God. Moses pointed to this promise from God in the following speech to the people of Israel:

> *¹ When all these blessings and curses I have set before you come on you and you take them to heart wherever the LORD your God disperses you among the nations, ² and when you and your children return to the LORD your God and obey him with all your heart and with all your soul according to everything I command you today, ³ then the LORD your God will restore your fortunes and have compassion on you and gather you again from all the nations where he scattered you. ⁴ Even if you have been banished to the most distant land under the heavens, from there the LORD your God will gather you and bring you back. ⁵ He will bring you to the land that belonged to your ancestors, and you will take possession of it. He will make you more prosperous and numerous than your ancestors. ⁶ The LORD your God will circumcise your hearts and the hearts of your descendants, so that you may love him with all your heart and with all your soul, and live. ⁷ The LORD your God will put all these curses on your enemies who hate and persecute you. ⁸ You will again obey the LORD and follow all his commands I am giving you today. ⁹ Then the LORD your God will make you most prosperous in all the work of your hands and in the fruit of your womb, the young of your livestock and the crops of your land. The LORD will again delight in you and make you prosperous, just as he delighted in your ancestors, ¹⁰ if you obey the LORD your God and keep his commands and decrees that are written in this Book of the Law and turn to the LORD your God with all your heart and with all your soul.*
>
> Deuteronomy 30:1–10

God fulfilled this promise to his people when he moved the heart of Cyrus of Persia—the people group who had conquered the Babylonians—to make a proclamation through his realm that said, "The LORD, the God of heaven, has given me all the kingdoms of the earth and he has appointed me to build a temple for him at Jerusalem in Judah. Any of his people among you may go up to Jerusalem in Judah and build the temple of the Lord, the God of Israel, the God who is in Jerusalem, and may their God be with them. And in any locality where survivors may now be living, the people are to provide them with silver and gold, with goods and livestock, and with freewill offerings for the temple of God in Jerusalem" (Ezra 1:2–4). He will also fulfill this promise in the regathering of Israel in the end times (see Jeremiah 32:37).

3. What does the Bible say were God's purposes for scattering his people? How were these purposes fulfilled in the Assyrian and Babylonian captivities?

4. What does it say about God's nature that he promised to regather his people even before they had entered into the Promised Land?

A Deliberate Purpose for Gathering

In the previous lesson, we noted that the apostle Paul wrote, "Christ himself gave the apostles, the prophets, the evangelists, the pastors and teachers, to equip his people for works of service, so that the body of Christ may be built up until we all reach unity in the faith and in the knowledge of the Son of God and become mature, attaining to the whole measure of the fullness of Christ" (Ephesians 4:11–13). The formation of the church reflects God's deliberate purpose in creating a space for worship, fellowship, accountability, and spiritual development. Jesus underscored the significance of this kind of community when he said the following:

> [15] "If your brother or sister sins, go and point out their fault, just between the two of you. If they listen to you, you have won them over. [16] But if they will not listen, take one or two others along, so that 'every matter may be established by the testimony of two or three witnesses.' [17] If they still refuse to listen, tell

it to the church; and if they refuse to listen even to the church, treat them as
you would a pagan or a tax collector.

[18] "Truly I tell you, whatever you bind on earth will be bound in heaven, and
whatever you loose on earth will be loosed in heaven.

[19] "Again, truly I tell you that if two of you on earth agree about anything
they ask for, it will be done for them by my Father in heaven. [20] For where two
or three gather in my name, there am I with them."

Matthew 18:15–20

Jesus emphasizes the divine presence that accompanies the communal worship of believers. The church, therefore, stands as a sacred assembly where individuals come together to honor God, engage in fellowship, and encounter the transformative influence of his presence. Furthermore, the New Testament illuminates the communal nature of the church as a platform for mutual support and spiritual advancement. We saw this in Ephesians 4:11–13, where Paul delineates the roles of spiritual gifts within the church—such as pastors, teachers, and leaders—aiming for the equipping of believers and the edification of the body of Christ.

The intentional gathering of believers in the church facilitates the sharing of spiritual gifts and allows believers to encourage and support one another. It creates an environment that is conducive to individual spiritual growth. So once again, we find that God's purpose for the church extends well beyond individual salvation to encompass the collective maturation and unity of believers as they navigate their spiritual journeys together. Essentially, the New Testament envisions the church as a dynamic community where God's intentions for gathering his people transcend mere congregational assembly to embrace spiritual development, community, and a shared experience of the Lord's grace.

5. What does Jesus say is the role of the church in pointing out a fault in a fellow believer? What does he say about the presence of God within the church?

6. What three outcomes among believers, as Paul states in Ephesians 4:11–16, are produced when the gathered church is operating as it should?

The Nature of the Church

One challenge we face in the community known as the body of Christ is that, while we are one with each other, it is impossible for us to know and relate to every person who has known and loved Jesus. Sure, we are all united together in our salvation, but we are not practically united with everyone in concrete relationships. Some members of the body of Christ lived long before we were born. Some who are alive today live in places around the world that we will never visit.

It is true that those who have traveled to remote destinations around the world testify to the unity they experienced with people who worshiped Jesus—even if they did so differently than they were used to doing. These short forays into other cultures serve to demonstrate the overall unity of God's people. But the fact remains that God's people are scattered around the world, which makes it difficult for us to experience this community in a tangible way.

This challenge has led people to distinguish two differing ways of referring to the church. The first is a reference to the *universal* church, comprised of all of God's people throughout all time and in all places. The second way of referring to the church—the one most commonly used in the Bible—is to the *local* church. In contrast to the universal church, the local church is comprised of a subset of individuals who have committed to consistent relationships and shared mission at a particular place. God gathers those who have been saved by his grace into local expressions of the church where he can be worshiped and his people can be conformed to his image. God sets up his local church with practices that are meant to foster the worship of his character and ensure that his people are spurred on toward holiness.

It is important to note that the local church shouldn't be confused with all who gather in a church building for worship on any given Sunday. These larger gatherings may be comprised of those who have not yet received God's salvation. They may be participating in the worship of the church but are not a part of the church—at least not yet. Additionally, on any given Sunday, churches will have those who are visiting from out of town or simply checking out the church. These people may be believers, and are thus a part of the universal church, but they have not committed to shared relationships and meaningful mission within that local body. This means that while the local church is always present, not all who are present will be a part of it.

We see this reality throughout the New Testament. In fact, the majority of the books in the New Testament are actually letters written to individual churches scattered throughout the Roman Empire. Each of these letters begins in a similar fashion, typically stating the author and then the community to whom it is written—which was most often a specific body of believers whom the author knew were gathering together to worship in a local church. We find various examples of this in the openings of the following New Testament books:

> [1] *Paul, an apostle of Christ Jesus by the will of God, to God's holy people in Ephesus, the faithful in Christ Jesus:* [2] *Grace and peace to you from God our Father and the Lord Jesus Christ.*
>
> Ephesians 1:1–2

> [1] *Paul and Timothy, servants of Christ Jesus, to all God's holy people in Christ Jesus at Philippi, together with the overseers and deacons:* [2] *Grace and peace to you from God our Father and the Lord Jesus Christ.*
>
> Philippians 1:1–2

> [1] *Paul, an apostle of Christ Jesus by the will of God, and Timothy our brother,* [2] *to God's holy people in Colossae, the faithful brothers and sisters in Christ: Grace and peace to you from God our Father.*
>
> Colossians 1:1–2

A few letters—such as 1 Timothy, 2 Timothy, and Titus—were written to specific individuals ministering in churches. Other letters—such as Galatians, James, and

Jude—appear to have been written to larger groups of believers or churches in a region. Regardless, the goal was to edify the local church, where people could be known, where they could use their gifts, and where they could mature under healthy teaching and leadership.

Sadly, many people never experience the joy of the local church. They might attend a church for a season, or rotate among a number of churches, but they never plant roots and commit to worshiping Jesus in a local community. The result is an isolated Christian life. People operating in this fashion might have relationships with other believers at varying times and in various places, but they miss out on the commitment found in the local church. For it is in the local church that we commit to serve one another, bear one another's burdens, reconcile in the face of conflict, give of our gifts, and partner together to pray, sing, and learn in community. This joint partnership allows for a collective experience of growth and transformation.

7. How would you describe what the difference is between the universal and the local church?

8. Are you a meaningful part of a local church? Why or why not? What are some ways that you are able to demonstrate commitment to your local church?

REFLECT

What can we conclude as to why God gathers believers together into what we call the church? Paul says the goal is for followers of Jesus to "grow to become in every respect the mature body of him who is the head, that is, Christ" (Ephesians 4:15). Jesus is the focus of the church. We are to grow and mature into the image of the one who has saved us and called us for his purposes. The gathered church shapes our love for Jesus in at least three ways.

First, the church intensifies our love for Jesus. Through the church, we are pressed "to know this love" of Christ "that surpasses knowledge," that we "may be filled to the measure of all the fullness of God" (Ephesians 3:19). The word *know* denotes more than mere intellect. It's experiential knowledge—the kind that would describe the way a husband knows his wife after a lengthy marriage. Passionate singing, authentic prayers, clear preaching, and the like are meant to help God's people experience the love of Christ intimately. And since people are prone to forget, this is not a one-time experience for the church. We don't experience love for Jesus and maintain that same intensity throughout our lives. We need the regular metronome of gathered worship to remind us of how great God's love is through Jesus Christ.

Second, the church strengthens our trust in Jesus. Think of this in terms of a weather report you see when a storm threatens to decimate a community. A reporter shows up and interviews people who are preparing their homes for what is to come. They are boarding up windows and securing objects that could be tossed by the wind or rain. This is what God's people do when they gather. The world around us is harsh. The onslaught of Satan and sin wreaks havoc. If we in the church are not prepared, the storm will crush us. So, as the local church of Christ, we gather around God's Word to continually remind ourselves of what is true, honorable, just, pure, lovely, commendable, excellent, and worthy of praise (see Philippians 4:8). Biblical teaching orients us to truth so that we are not "tossed back and forth by the waves" of the world (Ephesians 4:14). Baptism and the Lord's Supper also serve as ongoing practices in the church that help us to put the good news of Jesus on display.

And *third, the church is meant to equip our good works for Jesus.* In the church, we are allowed to discover how God has made us and our role in his mission. We use these gifts in the church to build up the body. We love, serve, and give of ourselves so that others will experience the love of Christ. These good works are not merely the things that exceptional leaders do in front of the people as they gather. We are all "created in Christ Jesus to do good works" (Ephesians 2:10), and these works can take many forms—such as serving so that the sound and video for the sermon work every week, or laboring to care for children during the service so that the adults can worship without distraction, or holding the doors, greeting guests, and showing people to their seats. The list goes on and on. These acts of service also equip those in the church to use their gifts in the world as they go about their lives each week.

9. How is your local church helping to intensify your love for Jesus? How, specifically, is your local church strengthening your trust in Jesus?

10. How is your local church equipping your good works for Jesus? What are some ways that you are currently serving others in your local church?

CLOSE

These three purposes—intensifying our love for Jesus, strengthening our trust in Jesus, and equipping our good works for Jesus—illuminate why we need the church. We can't accomplish these goals on our own. We were not designed to do so. So we can't just decide to tap out of the local church. We must stay engaged in the ongoing work of maturity in these areas until Jesus returns and our love for him is perfected, our trust in him becomes sight, and our good works are forever spent in perfect worship of our heavenly father.

It is worth leaning into the church. In spite of all its perceived and real blemishes, the church is God's plan for his work in the world. As Jesus declared to his disciple Peter,

"I tell you that you are Peter, and on this rock I will build my church, and the gates of Hades will not overcome it" (Matthew 16:18). This profound statement by Jesus underscores that the church is a cornerstone and fundamental aspect of God's strategy for his mission on earth. In fact, the very term *church* (*ekklesia* in Greek) signifies a purposeful assembly of believers, marking it as God's Plan A for advancing his kingdom. This designation goes beyond a mere human institution. It emphasizes the dynamic nature of the church rooted in the confession of Jesus as "the Messiah, the Son of the living God" (verse 16).

Jesus' proclamation depicts the church not as a passive entity but as an active force that is immune to the assaults of hell. It conveys the church in a proactive role of engaging in spiritual warfare and confronting the forces of darkness. God's primary plan thus involves a community of believers, empowered by the Holy Spirit, to actively participate in the mission of proclaiming the gospel, nurturing others in discipleship, and staunchly opposing the influences of evil. In this way, we in the church serve as a strategic instrument through which God's redemptive purposes unfold, dispelling darkness and establishing his rule on earth. It is within and through the church that God chooses to manifest his transformative work in the world.

11. What does Jesus reveal in Matthew 16:18 about the power and resilience of the church?

12. Why is it vital for believers to remain engaged in the mission of the church? What happens when believers "tap out" of their local congregation?

Lesson Three

GOD SCATTERS PEOPLE

"Now if you obey me fully and keep my covenant,
then out of all nations you will be my treasured possession.
Although the whole earth is mine, you will be for me a
kingdom of priests and a holy nation."

EXODUS 19:5–6

Live such good lives among the pagans that, though they
accuse you of doing wrong, they may see your good
deeds and glorify God on the day he visits us.

1 PETER 2:12

"Go into all the
world and
preach the gospel
to all creation."

MARK 16:15

WELCOME

Churches—particularly church buildings—have often been the center of life in a given community. From the earliest era of the church in North America, for instance, communities have tended to revolve around local congregations. Over time, these buildings become the epicenter for all sorts of activities ranging from civic to recreational.

In more recent history, as churches grew, so did their buildings. Churches began to create spaces that could accommodate the bustling activity incorporated throughout the week—offices where people could work, gyms where teams could play, cafés where people could drink coffee. Much of the life of the church took place in the building. This reality invariably created an association between the congregation of the church and the church building. Time spent in church buildings also promoted the notion that the primary work of the church took place when it gathered.

I grew up in a church that was reminiscent of this reality. If the church was open, our family was there. Sunday morning, Sunday night, and Wednesday night, the Coe family was in the building. We were even there on Monday night for outreach, Saturday for sports leagues, and during the day Monday through Friday for school. The church building was the catalyst for our community.

This is still the case in many pockets of culture. However, most people today spend far less time in physical church buildings during the week. They may attend a service once a week (or less) and perhaps connect with a small group at other times. Some of this is due to more people attending church virtually, which has made it possible for members to "attend church" without having to go into the building.[1] For others, the rapid pace of life means that they frequently miss worship with the gathered church. This leads to few hours spent with God's people to do the activities associated with the church—singing, praying, and preaching.

As in most everything in life, there are pros and cons to this new reality. The con is obvious. People need human connection, and there are many aspects of disciple-making that cannot happen without being "gathered" with one another in a church. However, there are some positive aspects of this new reality. The local church is no longer limited by a physical location. It can be in many places at one time. The reach of the church can extend to wherever its people are located. Thus, at least theoretically, the "scattered" church creates more opportunities for life-on-life ministry and outreach. The church has more of an opportunity to be on mission.

1. How often do you spend with the gathered church on a monthly basis? What are some of the ways that you physically connect with others in your church?

2. How have your gathering patterns changed over the years? Do you spend more or less time physically in a church building than you did a few years ago?

READ

More Scattered Than Gathered

The truth is that the church has always been more "scattered" than it has been "gathered." Local churches, at least in North America, have traditionally gathered on Sundays to meet together and highlight the significance of Jesus' resurrection. There are also many churches, like the one I attended growing up, where people regularly still meet together for many hours during the week. However, there are always more hours in the week when the local church is *not* gathered together. But this doesn't mean that the church stops being the church! It continues to be the church—even though its members are scattered among the world.

The authors of the New Testament reveal the dispersed nature of the early church, depicting it as a dynamic and decentralized entity with a presence in various geographical locations. Unlike a uniform and centrally governed institution, early Christian communities formed in diverse cities and regions, creating distinct local churches. Much of this initial "scattering" was prompted by a wave of persecution that broke out in the city of Jerusalem, where the first church had formed (see Acts 8:1–3). When this happened, "those who had been scattered preached the word wherever they went" (verse 4).

This eventually led to the establishment of churches, which first met in people's homes, in many cities throughout the known world. As noted in the previous lesson, we see this in the fact that Paul addressed many different congregations in his epistles—those in cities like Corinth, Thessalonica, and even Rome—and recognized the unique circumstances and challenges faced by each community. This scattered configuration of local churches reflected the flexible and adaptable nature of Christianity, which enabled it to take root in different cultural contexts while maintaining a common foundation of faith.

The decentralized structure of the local church in the New Testament also underscores the interconnectedness of its believers across various locations. Scholars note that Paul's letters, originally intended for specific congregations, were typically shared among different churches. The practice of sending messengers or delegates between these dispersed communities nurtured a sense of unity. In spite of the physical distances, there was a shared understanding of being part of a broader spiritual community, which emphasized the fact that the church transcended specific locations and formed a universal body of believers. This decentralized approach facilitated contextualization, celebrated diversity, and allowed for a dynamic expression of the gospel within different cultural settings, all of which served to contribute to the resilience and expansion of the early Christian movement.

All local churches thus exist in two shapes or forms: gathered and scattered. These two forms help us answer a key question: *What is the mission of the church?* Or, to state it more simply: *Why does the church exist?* In the following passage, the apostle Peter provides us with a picture of what the scattered church looks like and its purpose for being:

> ⁹ *But you are a chosen people, a royal priesthood, a holy nation, God's special possession, that you may declare the praises of him who called you out of darkness into his wonderful light.* ¹⁰ *Once you were not a people, but now you are the people of God; once you had not received mercy, but now you have received mercy.*
> ¹¹ *Dear friends, I urge you, as foreigners and exiles, to abstain from sinful desires, which wage war against your soul.* ¹² *Live such good lives among the pagans that, though they accuse you of doing wrong, they may see your good deeds and glorify God on the day he visits us.*
>
> 1 Peter 2:9–12

The descriptions of how God feels about his people are familiar if you've been journeying with us through the studies up to this point. "Chosen people." "Royal priesthood." "Holy nation." "God's special possession." These are the ways that God referred to the nation of Israel in the Old Testament. The Lord said to them, "If you obey me fully and keep my covenant, then out of all nations you will be my treasured possession. Although the whole earth is mine, you will be for me a kingdom of priests and a holy nation" (Exodus 19:5–6).

What is different about the description in 1 Peter 2:9–12 is that these concepts are now applied to all of God's people—Jew and Gentile alike—in the church. All of God's people have experienced his mercy and been gathered together as his church. The church gets the privilege of being his people. They are then sent into the word to "declare the praises of him" who called them "out of darkness into his wonderful light" (verse 9). Those outside the church are meant to see the good deeds of the church and "glorify God" (verse 12).

3. How did the "scattered" nature of the early church allow it to not only survive but actually thrive in a number of diverse places and cultures?

4. What similarities do you see between how God describes the people of Israel in the Old Testament and the people of the church in the New Testament?

God Uses His People

Peter therefore declares the twin tasks of the church as it scatters are to (1) speak about Jesus (see verse 9), and (2) show others who Jesus is through its members' distinct and separate lifestyles (see verse 12). In other words, the church is to declare and demonstrate the good news of Jesus. Christopher Wright, in his book *The Mission of God*, states the following:

> The whole earth, then, belongs to Jesus. It belongs to him by right of creation, by right of redemption and by right of future inheritance—as Paul affirms in

the magnificent cosmic declaration of Colossians 1:15–20. So wherever we go in his name, we are walking on his property. There is not an inch of the planet that does not belong to Christ. Mission then is an authorized activity carried out by tenants on the instructions of the owner of the property.[2]

It is helpful to note that God's plan of sending his people into the world to declare and demonstrate his glory has been his purpose ever since he created the world. Do you remember what he did back in the Garden of Eden? He first created a good world, then created Adam (followed by Eve), and then put them into the world and told them that they had work to do. They were meant to cultivate and care for God's created world so that his glory would fill the earth. God even gave Adam clear tasks like naming the animals (see Genesis 2:19). These were acts that God could have done himself, but he chose to use people to serve in his mission.

This same pattern continues throughout the Old Testament. For example, when God promised to free the Israelites from slavery in Egypt, he chose to use Moses. God did not have to use Moses. The God who could bring about the plagues and part the Red Sea did not require any person to do his bidding. But he *chose* to work through Moses. What's more, after Moses expressed doubt in his capabilities to accomplish God's mission, the Lord demonstrated that he always equips those whom he calls. He revealed that his selection is not based on human strength but on willingness to heed the divine call. Moses' journey shows how ordinary people, when yielded to God's purpose, can play extraordinary roles in his redemptive plans.

Another example is seen in the life of David, a shepherd who was unexpectedly anointed to be the king of Israel. David was overlooked by society, by his family, and even by the prophet Samuel. However, God said to his prophet, "The Lord does not look at the things people look at. People look at the outward appearance, but the Lord looks at the heart" (1 Samuel 16:7). It was David's heart that set him apart. God would go on to use David to defeat the giant Goliath and establish him as a significant leader in Israel's history.

These Old Testament narratives—in addition to many others—consistently reveal that God selects individuals for his purposes not because of their credentials but because of their faithfulness, obedience, and readiness to serve him for his glory.

God's choices are not based on conventional qualifications but on a person's character and devotion to him. The apostle Paul would later comment on this truth in a letter to the church in Corinth:

> [26] *Brothers and sisters, think of what you were when you were called. Not many of you were wise by human standards; not many were influential; not many were of noble birth.* [27] *But God chose the foolish things of the world to shame the wise; God chose the weak things of the world to shame the strong.* [28] *God chose the lowly things of this world and the despised things—and the things that are not—to nullify the things that are,* [29] *so that no one may boast before him.* [30] *It is because of him that you are in Christ Jesus, who has become for us wisdom from God—that is, our righteousness, holiness and redemption.* [31] *Therefore, as it is written: "Let the one who boasts boast in the Lord."*
>
> 1 Corinthians 1:26–31

The bottom line is that God uses people. Sometimes, when we look at the frailty and fallenness of humanity, we often wonder if God could have come up with a better plan! However, when we step back and think about it, we see that if God's ultimate goal is to proclaim his glory, then using humans in his mission makes perfect sense. It is in the brokenness and the inexperience that God's greatness shows through. So he chooses to use imperfect and seemingly ill-equipped people like Moses, David, and others to fulfill his tasks. As he does, he reveals that he is always faithful and that his plans will always prevail.

5. What was unusual, according to human standards, in God's choice to raise up Moses and David as leaders? What was God demonstrating by these selections?

6. What does Paul ask the believers to remember about themselves in 1 Corinthians 1:26–31? Why are they only to "boast in the Lord"?

God Empowers His People

Jesus continued the pattern that God set in the Old Testament. He could have announced the availability of God's kingdom in any way that he wanted. He could have announced his plan from the heavens or caused the rocks or mountains to cry out. But, once again, the choice was to work through people. Jesus called disciples (most of whom were uneducated) and apostles who would reveal God's mission through him to the world. He taught and modeled this message and then empowered his followers to preach his message and demonstrate his power:

> [1] After this the Lord appointed seventy-two others and sent them two by two ahead of him to every town and place where he was about to go. [2] He told them, "The harvest is plentiful, but the workers are few. Ask the Lord of the harvest, therefore, to send out workers into his harvest field. [3] Go! I am sending you out like lambs among wolves. [4] Do not take a purse or bag or sandals; and do not greet anyone on the road. . . ."
>
> [17] The seventy-two returned with joy and said, "Lord, even the demons submit to us in your name."
>
> [18] He replied, "I saw Satan fall like lightning from heaven. [19] I have given you authority to trample on snakes and scorpions and to overcome all the power of the enemy; nothing will harm you. [20] However, do not rejoice that the spirits submit to you, but rejoice that your names are written in heaven."
>
> [21] At that time Jesus, full of joy through the Holy Spirit, said, "I praise you, Father, Lord of heaven and earth, because you have hidden these things from the wise and learned, and revealed them to little children. Yes, Father, for this is what you were pleased to do."
>
> Luke 10:1–4, 17–21

The apostles (literally, "sent ones") extended the work of Jesus by doing what he did and saying what he said. Various signs and wonders testified to the fact that God was making all things new. Their active preaching helped people to understand that Jesus was the promised one who would fix the problem that sin had caused. Jesus would even later go so far as to say that his followers would do even greater works than he had done once he returned to heaven (see John 14:12). How amazing is that? God works through people to accomplish his mission.

7. What was Jesus' purpose in sending out the seventy-two ahead of him? What were they to ask the Lord to provide as they ministered?

8. How did Jesus respond to the report that he heard back from the seventy-two? What did he say that God has revealed to them and empowered them to do?

REFLECT

The church of today continues this pattern of service in God's mission. We are to continue to demonstrate the transformation that Jesus brings. Remember that in 1 Peter 2:12, we are told that the church's "good deeds" are meant to cause unbelievers to take notice. A bit later, Peter writes, "Always be prepared to give an answer to everyone who asks you to give the reason for the hope that you have" (1 Peter 3:15). This challenge assumes that we are living such distinct lives that others are asking about our source of strength and power. Christians function like road signs. Their lives are intended to point people to something and someone else. They help people see God and the change that he can bring in the lives of sinful men and women.

Of course, blank road signs are rarely helpful. We are meant to do more than simply point people to God through the godly way we lead our lives. We are also to speak the good news of Jesus. Paul makes this point when he writes, "We are therefore Christ's ambassadors, as though God were making his appeal through us. We implore you on Christ's behalf: Be reconciled to God" (2 Corinthians 5:20). This statement is so significant that we need to break it down a bit.

Notice that Paul is talking about all people who have been "reconciled" (or "made right") with God by virtue of Jesus' work. *Everyone* who knows Jesus has been commissioned to this task. And what is the task? We are to be Christ's ambassadors. Typically, this word is relegated to the political realm, where a person serves as an ambassador of one country to another country. The purpose of an ambassador is thus to represent one person or group to another, and an ambassador does this through his or her actions and words. All Christians who God has gathered into his church are his ambassadors. Even those who have just come to faith in Jesus are immediately given the mission of representing him by being his ambassador.

Furthermore, as Jesus' ambassadors, we are to "implore" others to come to Jesus. The word *implore* implies begging and pleading. Meaning, we are not simply to go about our own business and hope that somehow, in some way, people will see us and understand that Jesus is the true God. No! We speak up. We talk about Jesus with our friends, coworkers, neighbors, and family members—all the while longing that they would come to know Jesus as we do.

This is the mission of the scattered church. The job description of every Christian includes the work of demonstrating and declaring the gospel—and there is no opt-out clause. No earthly worker who wants to stay employed would ever imagine going to his or her boss and saying, "You know, that job description you gave me . . .

well, I like about 60 percent of it. But I'm not doing the other 40 percent." You would be looking for a new job within the hour!

We face the same responsibility in the job given to us by our Lord. We can't just sit back and say that we're in for the job of singing, or listening to sermons, or praying, or caring for other members in the church, but that we are unwilling to show and share the good news of Jesus Christ to a lost world. We must give ourselves to this mission.

9. What comes to mind when you hear the word *ambassador*? How are followers of Jesus to be like ambassadors who represent a person or group to the world?

10. What is Paul saying that your role or "job description" is when it comes to sharing about Christ? How are you currently fulfilling this mission?

CLOSE

As we conclude this lesson, remember that we are still talking about the work of the *local* church. It's easy to think that the work of evangelism and mission is the work of individual Christians . . . and this is true to a point. But, more importantly, this work is given to the local church. Together, we scatter into the world on active mission. Once there, we still function as a body, working together in harmony to see that the gospel gets to every person on the planet.

This work is part of God's plan for making all things right through Jesus. He is in control of all things and has "marked out [the] appointed times" that every person is alive, where every person lives, and the various other individuals whom every person will encounter (Acts 17:26). We might think that we chose the neighborhood where we live or the job where we would do meaningful work, or picked the gym we would join or restaurant we would frequent. Yet hovering behind all of this is the purpose and plan of God. He has appointed us to be his missionaries and ambassadors in those places. He has embedded those in his church in strategic locations where they can, uniquely, bring the truth of Jesus to bear.

As ambassadors, we work alongside other believers in these places. Believing co-workers labor with us in prayer and strategic witness to see to it that our colleagues hear the gospel. Friends from church partner with us in using our gifts strategically. We also divide and conquer. One believer, who is a bit more outspoken, might elect to share about Jesus, while another believer, who excels in compassion, might meet the needs of that person so that he or she can hear the message of Jesus without distraction. The church can also target specific agents of mission in the city, such as groups that work to care for vulnerable children or unwed mothers, and foster believers' interaction alongside healthy organizations.

Each church will do this work in unique ways. What is critical is that we take this mission seriously. We all need to fulfill the work of an ambassador as an act of worship to Jesus.

11. What are one or two reasons why God has you in the place where you currently are? What opportunities do you have to serve where you are as his ambassador?

12. What are some practical ways you can draw on the strengths of other believers in the church to accomplish God's mission in the world?

Notes

1. Thomas Costello, "17 Church Statistics for 2023 You Need to Know," Reach Right, October 28, 2023, https://reachrightstudios.com/church-statistics-2023/.
2. Christopher Wright, *The Mission of God* (Westmont, IL: InterVarsity Press, 2006).

GOD SENDS PEOPLE

"You shall have no other gods before me."

EXODUS 20:3

"Therefore go and make disciples of all nations, baptizing them in the name of the Father and of the Son and of the Holy Spirit, and teaching them to obey everything I have commanded you. And surely I am with you always, to the very end of the age."

MATTHEW 28:19–20

"Peace be with you!
As the Father
has sent me,
I am sending you."

JOHN 20:21

WELCOME

Have you ever been on a mission with a group? Not necessarily a mission *trip*—where you served at a place overseas—but a mission of any sort? In other words, have you ever set a goal with a group and then worked through the necessary steps to reach it?

We don't tend to think of "mission" in this way. But most of us have, at one time or another, been part of a group that had a clear goal the members were seeking to accomplish. Maybe it was a sports team trying to win a state championship, or a group at school striving to get a good grade on a collaborative project, or a team of employees at work attempting to close a big deal. These experiences help us to grasp the nature of mission. We strive to achieve a clearly defined goal that we truly believe matters by working with others.

People who are on mission are inspiring to us. Just consider the Wright brothers, who had a mission of seeing humans take to the air in flight. In their day, if a person wanted to get from New York to California, it took multiple days via train—and even longer by the other prevalent modes of transportation. But today, thanks to their invention of the airplane, you can travel cross-country in less than six hours. The Wright brothers' mission changed the way we live. In fact, most of us today just take airplane flights for granted.

A mission helps people understand where they are going, how they are going to get there, what their role is going to be in the process—and then rallies them to take action to achieve it. If the mission is not clear, the people involved will get frustrated and ultimately not be able to do anything meaningful. Additionally, if the mission is not inspiring, people will lack the motivation to move forward and, most likely, will lose interest along the way.

1. What are some significant missions that you have been on in your lifetime?

2. What are some of the key characteristics that made your missions successful (or not)?

READ

A Clearly Defined Goal

The church has a clearly defined goal. Its mission holds profound importance in shaping the spiritual landscape of individual lives and entire communities around the globe. At its core, the mission of the church is a call to action, encouraging believers to live out their faith and share the transformative message of Jesus Christ. Through acts of compassion, service, and evangelism, the church becomes a picture of Jesus to people everywhere. By actively engaging in the mission, the church fulfills its role as a "city on a hill" (see Matthew 5:14).

Additionally, the church's mission serves as a catalyst for personal growth and spiritual development. As believers participate in outreach and discipleship in their local churches and communities, they not only contribute to the well-being of others but also deepen their own faith. The mission of the church challenges them to live authentically and align their actions with Jesus, which in turn fosters a profound sense of purpose and fulfillment in them.

On a broader scale, the mission of the church contributes to the advancement of a more just and compassionate world. By addressing social issues and advocating for the well-being of all individuals, the church becomes a force for positive transformation. The mission underscores the importance of justice, mercy, and humility—values that resonate beyond religious boundaries and contribute to the common good. In essence, the church's mission is not just a theological concept but also a catalyst for change, both within the hearts of individuals and within the broader fabric of society. The following passages help us grasp this mission:

> [16] *Then the eleven disciples went to Galilee, to the mountain where Jesus had told them to go.* [17] *When they saw him, they worshiped him; but some doubted.* [18] *Then Jesus came to them and said, "All authority in heaven and on earth has been given to me.* [19] *Therefore go and make disciples of all nations, baptizing them in the name of the Father and of the Son and of the Holy Spirit,* [20] *and teaching them to obey everything I have commanded you. And surely I am with you always, to the very end of the age."*
>
> Matthew 28:16–20

> [3] *After [Jesus'] suffering, he presented himself to [his apostles] and gave many convincing proofs that he was alive. He appeared to them over a period of forty days and spoke about the kingdom of God.* [4] *On one occasion, while he was eating with them, he gave them this command: "Do not leave Jerusalem, but wait for the gift my Father promised, which you have heard me speak about.* [5] *For John baptized with water, but in a few days you will be baptized with the Holy Spirit."*
>
> [6] *Then they gathered around him and asked him, "Lord, are you at this time going to restore the kingdom to Israel?"*
>
> [7] *He said to them: "It is not for you to know the times or dates the Father has set by his own authority.* [8] *But you will receive power when the Holy Spirit comes on you; and you will be my witnesses in Jerusalem, and in all Judea and Samaria, and to the ends of the earth."*
>
> [9] *After he said this, he was taken up before their very eyes, and a cloud hid him from their sight.*
>
> [10] *They were looking intently up into the sky as he was going, when suddenly two men dressed in white stood beside them.* [11] *"Men of Galilee," they*

said, "why do you stand here looking into the sky? This same Jesus, who has been taken from you into heaven, will come back in the same way you have seen him go into heaven."

¹² Then the apostles returned to Jerusalem from the hill called the Mount of Olives, a Sabbath day's walk from the city.

Acts 1:3–12

From the Old Testament forward, we see that God is on a mission for God. His ultimate goal is for his name to be glorified and made famous—for people to revere him as the creator and sustainer of life. In the first of the Ten Commandments that he gave to his people, he clearly stated, "You shall have no other gods before me" (Exodus 20:3). Yet sadly, in the chapters of the Old Testament that follow, we see that God's people were quick to forget this command and often ended up worshiping the created over the creator.

3. What mission did Jesus give to his disciples in Matthew 28:16–20? What instructions did he then give them in Acts 1:3–12 about where they should go to make disciples?

4. In what ways have you seen the church contribute to the advancement of a more just and compassionate world? What roles do Christians play in bringing justice to people?

A Tale of Two Cities

This cosmic struggle of humankind wanting to do life their way as opposed to God's way is symbolized in the Old Testament in the missions of two cities. Throughout

Scripture, the cities of Jerusalem and Babylon are consistently demonstrated as having two different realities. Pastor James Boice notes, "Both Babylon and Jerusalem take on more than life-size dimensions and become symbols of two entirely different relationships to God and ways of life."[1]

From its beginning, Babylon was erected as a city with one goal—to make a name for itself. The Bible reveals that the city was built after the great flood of Noah's day, which had destroyed every city that existed before it (such as the city of Enoch mentioned in Genesis 4:17). We read of the origin of Babylon (also called Babel) in the following passage:

> ¹ Now the whole world had one language and a common speech. ² As people moved eastward, they found a plain in Shinar and settled there.
> ³ They said to each other, "Come, let's make bricks and bake them thoroughly." They used brick instead of stone, and tar for mortar. ⁴ Then they said, "Come, let us build ourselves a city, with a tower that reaches to the heavens, so that we may make a name for ourselves; otherwise we will be scattered over the face of the whole earth."
> ⁵ But the LORD came down to see the city and the tower the people were building. ⁶ The LORD said, "If as one people speaking the same language they have begun to do this, then nothing they plan to do will be impossible for them. ⁷ Come, let us go down and confuse their language so they will not understand each other."
> ⁸ So the LORD scattered them from there over all the earth, and they stopped building the city. ⁹ That is why it was called Babel—because there the LORD confused the language of the whole world. From there the LORD scattered them over the face of the whole earth.
>
> Genesis 11:1–9

Old Testament scholar Christopher Wright states, "The decision to settle and to build a city with a tower there seems to combine arrogance (in wanting to make a name for themselves) and insecurity (in wanting not to be scattered over the whole earth as God intended)."[2] The people of Babylon were showing, through their actions, that they were not relying on God for their well-being. The reality is that the people, by seeking a name for themselves, were placing themselves in direct competition with God.

The city of Jerusalem had an entirely different purpose. In Zechariah 1:14, God said that he was "very jealous" for Jerusalem. In 2 Kings 21:7, the Lord said, "In this temple and in Jerusalem, which I have chosen out of all the tribes of Israel, I will put my Name forever." In Isaiah 52:1, the prophet referred to Jerusalem as the "holy city." In Jeremiah 33:9, God said, "This city will bring me renown, joy, praise and honor before all nations on earth . . . [they] will tremble at the abundant prosperity and peace I provide for it." It was God's goal that what happened in the city be for his glory and ultimately have an impact on the surrounding nations.

The city of Jerusalem would ultimately serve as the launching pad of the missionary movement of the New Testament. In Acts 2, we read that it was a relatively small group of Jesus' followers who gathered together in the city at the time of Pentecost. But as a result of the Holy Spirit falling on those apostles, the church grew to more than three thousand people:

> *38 Peter replied [to the crowds], "Repent and be baptized, every one of you, in the name of Jesus Christ for the forgiveness of your sins. And you will receive the gift of the Holy Spirit. 39 The promise is for you and your children and for all who are far off—for all whom the Lord our God will call."*
>
> *40 With many other words he warned them; and he pleaded with them, "Save yourselves from this corrupt generation." 41 Those who accepted his message were baptized, and about three thousand were added to their number that day.*
>
> *42 They devoted themselves to the apostles' teaching and to fellowship, to the breaking of bread and to prayer. 43 Everyone was filled with awe at the many wonders and signs performed by the apostles. 44 All the believers were together and had everything in common. 45 They sold property and possessions to give to anyone who had need. 46 Every day they continued to meet together in the temple courts. They broke bread in their homes and ate together with glad and sincere hearts, 47 praising God and enjoying the favor of all the people. And the Lord added to their number daily those who were being saved.*
>
> Acts 2:38–47

The mission of God's people today is to live faithfully to him in this time and to make his name famous—not their own name famous, as the Babylonians sought to do.

All of this is to be done with an eager anticipation of the way that God has promised things ultimately to be. We read of this promise in the following passage: "We know that the whole creation has been groaning as in the pains of childbirth right up to the present time. Not only so, but we ourselves, who have the firstfruits of the Spirit, groan inwardly as we wait eagerly for our adoption to sonship, the redemption of our bodies" (Romans 8:22–23).

There is a longing in "the whole creation" for the renewal of all things—and God has promised to one day make all things right. So, as believers today, we are charged to live in our current "Jerusalem" and seek to bring glory to God by participating in his renewal purposes. All the while, we look forward to the "New Jerusalem," where everything will be forever made the way that it was originally intended to be (see Revelation 21:1–5).

5. What does the Genesis 11:1–9 passage reveal about why Babel/Babylon was founded? What was the goal of the people who constructed it?

6. What was different about the purpose of the city of Jerusalem? Why do you think God chose that place to be the launching pad for the church?

The What and Where Questions

Jesus' words in Matthew 28:16–20 answer the question of what we, as believers in the church, are to be doing. We are to "go and make disciples" for Jesus. The word *disciple* may seem a bit unfamiliar to us today, but it simply means to be a follower or student of Jesus. We are investing our lives to see others give their lives to loving

Jesus and living like him in the world. We do this by going out, baptizing, and teaching—three descriptions of the work of disciple-making. We go into the world on a strategic mission to declare and demonstrate the gospel.

As people come to faith in Jesus, they are baptized as a public testimony to God's work in their lives. We then walk with these new believers to help them understand God and his work in the world so that we, together, can obey all things that Jesus commanded. The bookends of this passage from Matthew are vital to this commission. Jesus says that he has "all authority in heaven and on earth" (verse 18). This means that he is the ruler of all and has the right to tell his people what to do. At the end of the passage, we read the amazing promise that his power goes into his people as they invest in the work of disciple-making. The work, while intimidating and risky, goes with the promise of the presence and power of God.

Jesus' words in Acts 1:8 then answer the question of where we, as believers in the church, should be making disciples. Remember that Jesus was making this appeal from Jerusalem, so the locations that he mentions are concentric circles radiating out from where he and the disciples were located. They were to start in Jerusalem, making disciples where they resided. They were then to spread out into the surrounding towns and villages (Judea), even going to places that were hostile and different (Samaria). Finally, the gospel was to extend to the ends of the earth through the witness of the church. God was sending his people, indwelt by the Holy Spirit, into the world to ensure that all people would hear the gospel message.

This language is reminiscent of the command that God gave Adam in the Garden of Eden when he told the first couple to be fruitful, multiply, and fill the earth:

> *26 Then God said, "Let us make mankind in our image, in our likeness, so that they may rule over the fish in the sea and the birds in the sky, over the livestock and all the wild animals, and over all the creatures that move along the ground."*
>
> *27 So God created mankind in his own image,*
> *in the image of God he created them;*
> *male and female he created them.*

²⁸ God blessed them and said to them, "Be fruitful and increase in number; fill the earth and subdue it. Rule over the fish in the sea and the birds in the sky and over every living creature that moves on the ground."

Genesis 1:26–28

Now, Jesus restates this commission and sends his people throughout the world to fill the earth with his glory. Think about it for a minute. The fact that some who are reading this study are Christians means that a portion of this commission has been fulfilled in our day. We are the ends of the earth from Jerusalem. The gospel came to us because faithful men and women lived with intentionality to declare and demonstrate the gospel to the ends of the earth. Now, we step into that great lineage and continue the work by taking the gospel further.

Those who have been reconciled to God are to be agents of reconciliation. They are responsible for bringing the hope of the gospel to others, starting where they are and extending to the ends of the earth. This is how each of us participates in the renewal of all things.

When most of us think about our role in God's mission, the problem usually isn't a lack of clarity about what we are supposed to be doing. We have an intuitive grasp that we should be pointing people to Jesus and leveraging our lives to make earth a bit more like heaven. Rather, for many of us the issue is one of priorities. We live busy lives with many distractions that crowd out intentionality in mission. Sadly, we're often guilty of just never getting around to the mission—particularly the mission of sharing Jesus with those who don't know him.

7. What about you? Is God's mission a priority in your life? How do you know?

8. Think through the concentric circles of your life. Who, where, or what types of people that God has asked you to reach fit in the following groups?

Jerusalem (those who are close to you and live where you do):

Judea (those who you are connected with in other places):

Samaria (those who are different from you and with whom you have clear differences):

Ends of the earth (a place or need around the world that God has placed on your heart):

REFLECT

The examples of mission we examined at the start of this lesson help us understand what it looks like when something really matters. Take a sports team, for instance. The mission is clear: win the championship. Those who make the team, particularly at higher levels of competition, clearly understand the importance of this mission. It matters to them. As a result, they do crazy things to prioritize the mission. They get up early to run a few miles or hit the gym. They discipline their bodies and refrain from eating certain foods so they are in peak condition. They suffer through practices day by day. The mission matters to them, and their lives show it.

This forces us to wrestle with the extent to which the Christian mission influences us and grips us at a heart level. In Matthew 9:35–38, we are given a unique glimpse into Jesus' heart for the mission. When he was ministering across the countryside, he looked over all the broken people and "had compassion on them." Why? Because they were "like sheep without a shepherd" (verse 36), which is another way of saying they were dead. Sheep without a shepherd will die, either of their own stupidity or at the hands of a predator. The same is true of people apart from Jesus. While they may seem to be peacefully moving through life, the reality is that they are doomed and destined for eternal separation from God (see Matthew 25:46; Ephesians 2:3; 2 Thessalonians 1:9). Their brokenness should move us deeply.

It certainly moved the apostle Paul. He wrote, "I . . . wish that I myself were cursed and cut off from Christ for the sake of my people, those of my own race" (Romans 9:3). Paul was willing to be cut off from God so that others, particularly the people of Israel, could experience salvation. His life's mission was for all people to hear the message of the gospel (see Acts 19:10). He lived to proclaim the gospel—that Jesus was God's answer for sin, that he died to pay the price for sin, that he rose victorious over sin, and that now, through faith, everyone can know God and experience his love. This was the message that oozed from Paul's life and defined his identity. He understood that the mission truly mattered.

Paul called others to follow in this same pattern. As he wrote later in his letter to the church in Rome, "How, then, can they call on the one they have not believed in? And how can they believe in the one of whom they have not heard? And how can they hear without someone preaching to them?" (Romans 10:14). The answer to Paul's question about how those who need the gospel will hear it is the same as the way people hear about anything. Someone has to tell them. We hear about a political candidate because people talk. We hear a famous musician sing and friends start talking. An actress completes an amazing performance and people talk it up, in person and online. People hear about Jesus in the same way—those who know him talk about him. Sent ones go and preach the message.

Don't let the language Paul uses of "preaching" be a stumbling block for you. We tend to think of preaching as something that a certain person does when the church gathers. This is certainly preaching, but it is not the only form preaching takes. We are preaching any time we share the message of Jesus with others, whether we do that in a large group, or over lunch with our neighbor, or with a friend at a restaurant. We are the means by which others hear.

This extends beyond just the locations where we live. For the world to hear, people must go and tell them. Missions is as necessary today as it ever was—whether that is people uprooting their lives from a picket-fence existence to plant a church in an inner-city context or someone moving to a poverty-stricken community in a developing nation. There are still many places around the world with inadequate access to the gospel message and without healthy churches where they can grow in their faith. The church needs people who are willing to sacrifice everything to take the gospel to places where Jesus is not yet known.

9. To what extent does the Christian mission grip you at a heart level? Would you say you feel the same about the lost as Jesus and Paul felt about them? Explain your response.

10. Does the idea of preaching to others intimidate you? What are some practical and nonthreatening ways that you could "preach" the gospel this week?

CLOSE

The simple "sent-ness" of the church happens through the church. The work of disciple-making to the nations is at the core of the church's identity. It is tempting to think that the mission is one small piece of the work of the local church—alongside the music, the children's ministry, and the rest—but it's more accurate to see everything the church does as its mission. We preach, pray, care for kids, and greet people who attend our weekly service—and the host of other activities in the church—because we long for people to know and love Jesus.

All of us in the church have our own unique role to play in this mission. We work together with one another to make Jesus known. This is the way Jesus worked during his earthly ministry. He commissioned the apostles to travel in groups and partner together in the grand mission. The same is true of the early church. The first missionaries worked in strategic teams of complementary individuals to accomplish the mission. Today's local churches continue this pattern by aligning for mission. The leaders equip the body of believers in the church for this mission through ongoing teaching and equipping as well as strategic decisions regarding the nature and locations of missionary work around the world. Shared mission is another key reason why God's people need the local church. We can truly do more together.

11. In your own words, how would you define the mission of the church?

12. Why do the nations matter to God? In what ways is your local church involved in what the Lord is doing in the nations around the world?

Notes

1. James Boice, *Two Cities, Two Loves* (Westmont, IL: InterVarsity Press, 1996), 5.
2. Christopher Wright, *The Mission of God* (Westmont, IL: InterVarsity Press, 2006), 196.

Lesson Five

GOD CONNECTS PEOPLE

So the wall was completed on the twenty-fifth of Elul,
in fifty-two days.

NEHEMIAH 6:15

Therefore, as we have opportunity,
let us do good to all people, especially to those
who belong to the family of believers.

GALATIANS 6:10

Do good . . . be rich
in good deeds . . .
be generous and
willing to share.

1 TIMOTHY 6:18

WELCOME

Up to this point, the focus of this study has been on the outward face of the church to the world. But in the final two lessons, we will shift the focus to the internal relationships that people have within the church. This order is intentional. As followers of Jesus, we are naturally prone to focus more on internal aspects of church life. The church gathering and the people who make up our church family are central to our experience, so they tend to dominate our thoughts when we think about who the church is and what it does. But as we saw in the previous lesson, God's mission to bring the gospel to the ends of the earth is central to what the church does. Everything is about people coming to know and love Jesus and grow as his followers.

Now that we have put the mission of the church in its proper perspective, it is important to recognize that the church is—as we discussed previously—a body. It is a body made up of many parts, with each being interconnected and interdependent. The bottom line is that we need one another. No individual can be all that God intended him or her to be without the help of others. In fact, there are at least two reasons why we need each other in the church.

First, none of the gifts and talents that we have as individuals work in a vacuum. We need the gifts of others in order for our own gifts to be fully maximized. For instance, if you have the gift of hospitality—the gift of serving others and making them feel welcome—that gift needs to be complemented by someone with a gift of administration. You need someone who can make sure all the supplies are ordered, the rooms are reserved, and the budget is set. The reality is that if you are gifted in an area, you are probably passionate about things that other people find burdensome or difficult (and vice versa). We need each other to carry the things we find wearisome.

Second, we need each other so that we can be all that God intends for us to be. The Bible says, "As iron sharpens iron, so one person sharpens another" (Proverbs 27:17).

We need each other so that we can be "sharpened." This is the antithesis of our modern-day mindset that says a person should be self-made and not depend on anyone else. However, as followers of Jesus, we know that if we have the right people around us, they will make us better. Even if they are holding us accountable and calling out flaws, in the end—if the other person has our best interests in mind—their accountability should be a welcome asset in our lives. Throughout this lesson, we are going to discover God's design for interconnectedness in the church.

1. What are some gifts that you believe God has given you to contribute to the church? How have you worked with others in the church to maximize those gifts?

2. What are some ways that others in the church have helped you "sharpen" your faith? How has God used you as his instrument to "sharpen" others?

READ

The Power of Connection

When God first called Abram to follow him, the Lord promised him, "I will make you into a great nation, and I will bless you" (Genesis 12:2). The descendants of Abram became God's "chosen people," the Israelites, who were given the mission of carrying out the Lord's purposes in the world. On one hand, this nation embodied what it meant to seek after God and pursue him with a whole heart. But on the other hand, they also modeled what it looks like to rebel against God's purposes and pursue one's own selfish desires. In the end, Israel rose together, fell together, and then rose again together.

One of the places where we see the interconnectedness of the Israelites on display is in the book of Nehemiah. In this story, we get a glimpse of the people being on the rise together. In 586 BC, the nation of Judah was conquered by the Babylonians. The wall around the city of Jerusalem was broken down, the temple and other important buildings set ablaze, and the inhabitants taken into exile (see 2 Kings 25:8–11). But now, years later, the Lord had provided a way for the city to be renewed. Nehemiah was chosen to be one of the rebuilders.

Nehemiah's immediate task was to rebuild the wall around the city—a feat that had been attempted by others before him but had not been accomplished. In fact, it was a report about some of those failures that prompted Nehemiah to first seek the Lord and then go to the king to ask if he could lead the rebuilding efforts (see Nehemiah 1:3–2:8). When the king granted Nehemiah's request, he knew that the gracious hand of God was on him (see 2:8) and that the Lord had chosen him to fulfill this task. Still, it remained a huge endeavor. The wall around the city of Jerusalem was two-and-a-half miles long and made of heavy stone. Without the aid of modern machinery, it would have been a daunting and labor-intensive job.

This is where the interconnectedness of God's people comes into play. Nehemiah understood that the massive wall around the city could only be rebuilt if God's people united together in one purpose. Nehemiah also understood this had to be done quickly to protect the people of Jerusalem from attacks from their enemies. So he said to the people, "You see the trouble we are in: Jerusalem lies in ruins, and its gates have been burned with fire. Come, let us rebuild the wall of Jerusalem, and we will no longer be in disgrace" (2:17). The following passage from the next chapter in Nehemiah relates what happened next:

> ¹ *Eliashib the high priest and his fellow priests went to work and rebuilt the Sheep Gate. They dedicated it and set its doors in place, building as far as the Tower of the Hundred, which they dedicated, and as far as the Tower of Hananel.* ² *The men of Jericho built the adjoining section, and Zakkur son of Imri built next to them.*
> ³ *The Fish Gate was rebuilt by the sons of Hassenaah. They laid its beams and put its doors and bolts and bars in place.* ⁴ *Meremoth son of Uriah, the son of Hakkoz, repaired the next section. Next to him Meshullam son of Berekiah,*

the son of Meshezabel, made repairs, and next to him Zadok son of Baana also made repairs. ⁵ The next section was repaired by the men of Tekoa, but their nobles would not put their shoulders to the work under their supervisors.

⁶ The Jeshanah Gate was repaired by Joiada son of Paseah and Meshullam son of Besodeiah. They laid its beams and put its doors with their bolts and bars in place. ⁷ Next to them, repairs were made by men from Gibeon and Mizpah—Melatiah of Gibeon and Jadon of Meronoth—places under the authority of the governor of Trans-Euphrates. ⁸ Uzziel son of Harhaiah, one of the goldsmiths, repaired the next section; and Hananiah, one of the perfume-makers, made repairs next to that. They restored Jerusalem as far as the Broad Wall. ⁹ Rephaiah son of Hur, ruler of a half-district of Jerusalem, repaired the next section. ¹⁰ Adjoining this, Jedaiah son of Harumaph made repairs opposite his house, and Hattush son of Hashabneiah made repairs next to him. ¹¹ Malkijah son of Harim and Hasshub son of Pahath-Moab repaired another section and the Tower of the Ovens. ¹² Shallum son of Hallohesh, ruler of a half-district of Jerusalem, repaired the next section with the help of his daughters.

¹³ The Valley Gate was repaired by Hanun and the residents of Zanoah. They rebuilt it and put its doors with their bolts and bars in place. They also repaired a thousand cubits of the wall as far as the Dung Gate.

¹⁴ The Dung Gate was repaired by Malkijah son of Rekab, ruler of the district of Beth Hakkerem. He rebuilt it and put its doors with their bolts and bars in place.

¹⁵ The Fountain Gate was repaired by Shallun son of Kol-Hozeh, ruler of the district of Mizpah. He rebuilt it, roofing it over and putting its doors and bolts and bars in place. He also repaired the wall of the Pool of Siloam, by the King's Garden, as far as the steps going down from the City of David. ¹⁶ Beyond him, Nehemiah son of Azbuk, ruler of a half-district of Beth Zur, made repairs up to a point opposite the tombs of David, as far as the artificial pool and the House of the Heroes.

¹⁷ Next to him, the repairs were made by the Levites under Rehum son of Bani. Beside him, Hashabiah, ruler of half the district of Keilah, carried out repairs for his district. ¹⁸ Next to him, the repairs were made by their fellow Levites under Binnui son of Henadad, ruler of the other half-district of Keilah. ¹⁹ Next to him, Ezer son of Jeshua, ruler of Mizpah, repaired another section, from a point facing the ascent to the armory as far as the angle of the wall.

²⁰ Next to him, Baruch son of Zabbai zealously repaired another section, from the angle to the entrance of the house of Eliashib the high priest. ²¹ Next to him, Meremoth son of Uriah, the son of Hakkoz, repaired another section, from the entrance of Eliashib's house to the end of it.

²² The repairs next to him were made by the priests from the surrounding region. ²³ Beyond them, Benjamin and Hasshub made repairs in front of their house; and next to them, Azariah son of Maaseiah, the son of Ananiah, made repairs beside his house. ²⁴ Next to him, Binnui son of Henadad repaired another section, from Azariah's house to the angle and the corner, ²⁵ and Palal son of Uzai worked opposite the angle and the tower projecting from the upper palace near the court of the guard. Next to him, Pedaiah son of Parosh ²⁶ and the temple servants living on the hill of Ophel made repairs up to a point opposite the Water Gate toward the east and the projecting tower. ²⁷ Next to them, the men of Tekoa repaired another section, from the great projecting tower to the wall of Ophel.

Nehemiah 3:1–27

Under Nehemiah's leadership—and with the Lord's help—the wall around Jerusalem was rebuilt in only fifty-two days (see Nehemiah 6:15). This is all the more astounding when we consider the fact that the people were under constant attack by their enemies and had to divert some of their efforts to protecting those who were doing the work (see 4:7–14). In the end, the story reveals that when God's people work together in his power, great things can happen.

3. Reread the passage in Nehemiah 3:1–27 and circle each team that was formed to complete the task of rebuilding the wall. How many teams did you find?

4. What were some of the different roles that each team played?

Carrying Each Other's Burdens

In previous lessons, we have examined how God's mission for the church is for believers to work together to ensure that every person on earth has the chance to see, hear, and respond to the gospel of Jesus. This partnership in mission is vital. However, there are other ways that believers are to partner together to become more like Jesus and fulfill their mission. The following passage helps us understand such relationships we are to have within the church:

> [1] *Brothers and sisters, if someone is caught in a sin, you who live by the Spirit should restore that person gently. But watch yourselves, or you also may be tempted.* [2] *Carry each other's burdens, and in this way you will fulfill the law of Christ.* [3] *If anyone thinks they are something when they are not, they deceive themselves.* [4] *Each one should test their own actions. Then they can take pride in themselves alone, without comparing themselves to someone else,* [5] *for each one should carry their own load.* [6] *Nevertheless, the one who receives instruction in the word should share all good things with their instructor.*
>
> [7] *Do not be deceived: God cannot be mocked. A man reaps what he sows.* [8] *Whoever sows to please their flesh, from the flesh will reap destruction; whoever sows to please the Spirit, from the Spirit will reap eternal life.* [9] *Let us not become weary in doing good, for at the proper time we will reap a harvest if we do not give up.* [10] *Therefore, as we have opportunity, let us do good to all people, especially to those who belong to the family of believers.*
>
> Galatians 6:1–10

The churches in Galatia to whom Paul was addressing this letter were divided in many ways. Evidently, teachers had arrived in the region who were throwing them into confusion and "trying to pervert the gospel of Christ" (Galatians 1:7). These teachers were telling the people in Paul's churches—most of whom were Gentiles—that they had to keep to the Jewish ceremonial laws of the Old Testament in order to be considered a Christian. The fact that the congregations were buying into this idea prompted Paul to declare, "I am astonished that you are so quickly deserting the one who called you to live in the grace of Christ and are turning to a different gospel—which is really no gospel at all" (verses 6–7). Paul wrote to show them the unity that was theirs through the work of Christ. His grace had united all people in one family.

In Galatians 6:1–10, Paul revealed what this type of family should look like in practical terms. The first thing to notice about this passage is that Paul assumed that all people would experience burdens. Everyone has them; no one is immune. Some of these burdens come from within—our sin, past history, or fallen personality. Other burdens come from the outside—things that happen to us or the evils we experience simply by living in a world broken by sin. It is amazing to think about the sheer amount of burdens that enter a church building each time the church gathers. Pain is a great equalizer among all people.

What was Paul's answer to the burdens of life? Other people. At least in part, the answer to a sin-broken world is healthy, burden-bearing relationships with those who love and follow Jesus. In another letter, Paul told a church, "Do nothing out of selfish ambition or vain conceit. Rather, in humility value others above yourselves, not looking to your own interests but each of you to the interests of the others" (Philippians 2:3–4). Paul's point is that God has called the church to bear one another's burdens. It is not a request but a command.

5. What are some ways that the interconnected church serves its members?

6. How have you personally seen the church "carry the burdens" of others?

Burden-Bearing Relationships

Going back to the image of the church as a body is helpful here. The apostle Paul wrote of the church, "We were all baptized by one Spirit so as to form one body—whether Jews or Gentiles, slave or free—and we were all given the one Spirit to drink. Even so the body is not made up of one part but of many" (1 Corinthians 12:13–14). Paul goes on to note that each individual part of the body—the foot, the hand, the eye, the ear, the nose—are necessary for the entire body to function as it was intended. He then states the following:

> ¹⁸ *But in fact God has placed the parts in the body, every one of them, just as he wanted them to be.* ¹⁹ *If they were all one part, where would the body be?* ²⁰ *As it is, there are many parts, but one body.*
>
> ²¹ *The eye cannot say to the hand, "I don't need you!" And the head cannot say to the feet, "I don't need you!"* ²² *On the contrary, those parts of the body that seem to be weaker are indispensable,* ²³ *and the parts that we think are less honorable we treat with special honor. And the parts that are unpresentable are treated with special modesty,* ²⁴ *while our presentable parts need no special treatment. But God has put the body together, giving greater honor to the parts that lacked it,* ²⁵ *so that there should be no division in the body, but that its parts should have equal concern for each other.* ²⁶ *If one part suffers, every part suffers with it; if one part is honored, every part rejoices with it.*
>
> ²⁷ *Now you are the body of Christ, and each one of you is a part of it.*
>
> 1 Corinthians 12:18–27

Notice Paul's comment that "if one part suffers, every part suffers with it" (verse 26). In the same way that our entire body will struggle if one part of it is suffering—such as enduring the pain of a broken ankle or hand—so the whole body of Christ will struggle when one of its members is suffering. For this reason, the burden-bearing relationships in the church necessitate that we must act in order to show care for others. As John says, "Let us not love with words or speech but with actions and in truth" (1 John 3:18).

Active love must be practiced within the church—particularly to those who are burdened and oppressed. This is not to suggest that there is a certain subset of Christians who are mature, not burdened, and therefore called to bear with weaker Christians. Rather, the assumption is that all people in the church are going to be burdened in unique ways, and in different seasons of life, and are all going to stand in need of burden-bearing relationships.

7. What does Paul's illustration of the church as a "body" reveal about God's intentions for the church when it comes not only to using spiritual gifts but also sharing burdens?

8. Paul reveals that sharing one another's burdens should be the normal pattern in the church. Why do you think this does not happen more often?

REFLECT

There are two unique obstacles worth noting when it comes to why we don't see more burden-bearing relationships in the church. The first is self-righteousness, which causes people to try and look better than they actually are and refrain from allowing others into their lives. This can happen when people maintain a superficial connection to the church. They attend church periodically, stand at a distance, and fail to engage in long-term relationships. It can also happen when people strive to care for the needs of others in an effort to justify themselves and make it appear they are not in need of the same type of burden-bearing. They want others to think they have it all together, so they keep everything in the dark until it all falls apart.

A second impediment is selfishness. Burdens are called "burdens" for a reason. It is often simply easier for people in the church to stand back and not engage when others are experiencing pain. Most people have enough burdens of their own, and the thought of willingly getting into the burdens of others and taking them on is a prospect they would rather avoid. Burden-bearing will, by its very definition, bleed time, energy, emotion, money, and predictability from our lives. We have to make our lives more difficult in order to care well.

However, when it comes to each of these obstacles, we have to remember that burden-bearing follows the model set by Jesus Christ (see Ephesians 4:32). He is the supreme example of one who did not look out for his own interests but gave of himself sacrificially for others. As John wrote, "We love because he first loved us" (1 John 4:19). Those who have been the recipient of Jesus' love are compelled to willingly extend this type of love to others.

But for this type of love to happen, it must be a priority among those who make up the church. It is simply not enough to come to the church building each week, be encouraged by the music and teaching, and then leave without developing mean-ingful relationships. This would be like eating a meal on Sunday and then trusting that the nutrition from that meal would last the whole week! We were not designed to live that way, nor were we created to relegate our Christian community to one time each week. We need ongoing relationships.

This means that we must make church attendance a priority. In order to know and be known, we have to show up. The author of Hebrews made this point to his readers when he wrote, "Let us consider how we may spur one another on toward love and good deeds, not giving up meeting together, as some are in the habit of doing, but encouraging one another—and all the more as you see the Day approaching" (Hebrews 10:24–25). We show up so we can consider others. The church isn't all about us. It's about how God can use us to impact others.

Burden-bearing relationships will also require vulnerability. We have to be willing to drag ourselves out of darkness and live in the light (see 1 John 1:5–10). Not only should we confess our sins to God, but we should also talk with others about our sin and let them in on our points of weakness. Paul modeled this type of confession, as he regularly spoke of his weakness to others (see 1 Corinthians 2:3; 2 Corinthians 4:8–9; 12:9). This takes incredible humility in a world that prizes maintaining an image of polished perfection, but the work of confession is vital to genuine growth. We need others who know us, pray for us, speak truth to us, and press us to holiness in specific areas. If others know us well enough to know where we struggle, then we have built a community that can help us strive for holiness in all areas. To fail to bring others into our lives is to neglect one of the most beautiful gifts that God has given to his church.

9. Which of the two obstacles—self-righteousness or selfishness—most commonly gets in the way of you developing healthy burden-bearing relationships? Explain your response.

10. Are you truly known by others in your church? What is one tangible step you could take this week to deepen the quality of the relationships you have with God's people?

CLOSE

A primary way that we live in community with others in the church is through prayer. As people let us into their lives, and we allow them to know us, we are able to pray for specific needs. Paul's letters to the churches, in fact, were a steady stream of such prayer requests. The apostle James also commended this model to the church:

"Confess your sins to each other and pray for each other so that you may be healed. The prayer of a righteous person is powerful and effective" (James 5:16). Followers of Jesus in the church should pray regularly for one another, knowing that God has seen fit to work through the prayers of his people.

Beyond prayer, we should model practical support for other Christians. This could simply take the form of being a good listener by coming alongside others in their pain. We comfort, cry with, care for, and console the person. Other times, we might need to call out sin in others. We can graciously and kindly point out blind spots in their lives and help them work to address those areas of needed growth. We are called to "encourage one another daily . . . so that none of [us] may be hardened by sin's deceitfulness" (Hebrews 3:13). Since we love others and don't want to see them fall into sin, we actively press them to repent and follow Christ. The most unloving thing to do would be to turn a blind eye to the sin of those we love.

Another way that we live well in community is by working through conflicts in a healthy and honoring way. Given that we "all have sinned" (Romans 3:23), conflicts are unavoidable in our relationships. We may be tempted to not work through such turmoil and merely distance ourselves from the person (or move to another nearby church). But when we make that choice, we miss out on a primary method that God uses to grow us into maturity. The church is often the instrument God uses to help us work through our conflicts according to his standards. We learn to admit when we are wrong instead of holding on to our pride. We quickly forgive others when they do wrong to us and seek forgiveness from others when we wrong them. We refuse to hold on to grudges and instead seek to find common ground with each other. We learn how to "not be quarrelsome" but "kind to everyone . . . not resentful" (2 Timothy 2:24).

Finally, we should find ways to tangibly encourage others by meeting their needs. We are called to "share with the Lord's people who are in need" (Romans 12:13) and "share with others" (Hebrews 13:16). We are to live in sacrificial relationships where we sacrifice what we have for the sake of the common good. In doing this, we follow the model of the early church, where the believers "sold property and possessions to give to anyone who had need," with the result that "the Lord added to their number daily those who were being saved" (Acts 2:45, 47).

11. On a scale of 1–5, with 1 being poor and 5 being excellent, how would you rank your present engagement in each of these areas?

Listening to others

1   2   3   4   5

Praying for others

1   2   3   4   5

Challenging others to not sin

1   2   3   4   5

Reconciling conflicts with others

1   2   3   4   5

Meeting the needs of others

1   2   3   4   5

12. When is a time that someone in the church came alongside you in a season of particular need? What was that experience like for you?

Lesson Six

GOD GIFTS PEOPLE

*Then the Lᴏʀᴅ said to Moses, "See, I have chosen
Bezalel son of Uri, the son of Hur, of the tribe of Judah,
and I have filled him with the Spirit of God, with wisdom,
with understanding, with knowledge and with
all kinds of skills."*

EXODUS 31:1–3

*Now to each one the manifestation of the Spirit
is given for the common good.*

1 CORINTHIANS 12:7

Every good and perfect

gift is from

above, coming down

from the Father.

JAMES 1:17

WELCOME

If you are part of the church, you have a role to play in the world. God has uniquely wired each of us to add value, serve others, solve problems, and accomplish many other things for his kingdom. In a real sense, if we are not using our gifts as God intended, the world is missing out on our contribution. This would be a great travesty!

However, the problem is that many followers of Jesus either misunderstand their gifts or have not been given a great model by the church on how to exercise their gifts. If we were to observe the average church on most Sundays, we would be left with the impression that the gifts needed in the church are (1) communication (preaching and teaching), (2) singing/musicianship (worship leading), (3) logistics (parking cars, organizing volunteers), and (4) hospitality (making people feel welcome by greeting them). Of course, this oversimplifies the situation a bit. But don't miss the main point: the gifts on display on Sunday morning, in the average church, are not the totality of the gifts that God has given to the church.

As I mentioned in a previous lesson, I grew up in a traditional church. For the most part, I loved everything about my childhood church experience. However, I do not remember receiving much (if any) teaching or modeling on the diversity of gifts that God gives the church. My experience was reflective of what I described: going to church whenever the doors were open, participating in church sports leagues, engaging in community. I came away with the impression that only a handful of gifts were for the church and the rest were somehow "secular" or for the world. It wasn't until I was older and had gained a deeper understanding that I realized that the sacred/secular divide of gifts in the church does not exist in Scripture.

Abraham Kuyper, a prominent theologian and prime minister of the Netherlands from 1901 to 1905, once wrote, "There is not a square inch in the whole domain of our human existence over which Christ, who is Sovereign over all, does not cry:

'Mine!'"[1] In other words, God is sovereign over all things—there is no such thing as the sacred/secular divide.

The gifts that God has given you to serve the world are the same that he has given you to further his kingdom through the church. So, if you are an entrepreneur, God wants you to use those gifts to expand his fame among the nations. If you are administratively minded, he wants you to use those gifts to help organize kingdom activities. I could go on and on. The bottom line is that God has wired you to make a difference in the world through his church and for his glory.

1. What types of gifts do you see being used in your church on a typical Sunday? What are some other gifts that might be at work "behind the scenes"?

2. Take another look at the above quote from Abraham Kuyper. How does this re-shape the way you think about the application of the gifts you have been given?

READ

Everyone Matters

Everyone matters may sound like one of those trite clichés you read on a coffee mug or rustic sign. But it's true—particularly in the church.

We can validate the point by building a case based on Scripture. The Bible tells us that God gives his Spirit to his disciples (see John 20:22). Paul states that a person who becomes a Christian is sealed with the Holy Spirit (see Ephesians 1:13). The Spirit of God is the sign, or seal, that someone has been saved by Jesus. Christians can quench the Spirit's work in their lives through sinful actions (see 1 Thessalonians 5:19). Like a water hose with a crimp in it, those who continue to nurture sin and fail to repent limit the flow of the Spirit's activity in their lives. Yet God's Spirit remains—he will not take away his Spirit from his people (see Ephesians 4:30).

The Spirit of God is given to the people of God for a number of purposes. The Holy Spirit comforts God's people in an evil world (see John 14:26). The Holy Spirit convicts the world of sin, God's righteousness, and the Lord's coming judgment (see John 16:8). The Holy Spirit empowers the disciples of Jesus for the mission of the church (see Acts 1:8). The Spirit of God also gifts the people of God for ministry. We see this in the following passages from Paul:

> [1] *Now about the gifts of the Spirit, brothers and sisters, I do not want you to be uninformed.* [2] *You know that when you were pagans, somehow or other you were influenced and led astray to mute idols.* [3] *Therefore I want you to know that no one who is speaking by the Spirit of God says, "Jesus be cursed," and no one can say, "Jesus is Lord," except by the Holy Spirit.*
> [4] *There are different kinds of gifts, but the same Spirit distributes them.* [5] *There are different kinds of service, but the same Lord.* [6] *There are different kinds of working, but in all of them and in everyone it is the same God at work.*
> [7] *Now to each one the manifestation of the Spirit is given for the common good.* [8] *To one there is given through the Spirit a message of wisdom, to another a message of knowledge by means of the same Spirit,* [9] *to another faith by the same Spirit, to another gifts of healing by that one Spirit,* [10] *to another miraculous powers, to another prophecy, to another distinguishing between spirits, to another speaking in different kinds of tongues, and to still another the interpretation of tongues.* [11] *All these are the work of one and the same Spirit, and he distributes them to each one, just as he determines.*
>
> 1 Corinthians 12:1–11

> [5] *So in Christ we, though many, form one body, and each member belongs to all the others.* [6] *We have different gifts, according to the grace given to each of us. If your gift is prophesying, then prophesy in accordance with your faith;*

7 if it is serving, then serve; if it is teaching, then teach; 8 if it is to encourage, then give encouragement; if it is giving, then give generously; if it is to lead, do it diligently; if it is to show mercy, do it cheerfully.

Romans 12:5–8

There is no indication that these lists are meant to be exhaustive, as if they record every way the Spirit gifts God's people for mission. They are more likely a representative sample of common gifts. Also, it's not as if each person is given only one gift. Some may have a number of these gifts at work. Regardless, Paul notes that the reason for gifting is the same: "Now to each one the manifestation of the Spirit is given for the common good" (1 Corinthians 12:7).

3. What are some of the reasons as to why God gives his Spirit to people?

4. What are some of the gifts that Paul lists in 1 Corinthians 12:1–11 and Romans 12:5–8? What similarities and difference do you observe between the lists?

A Divine Purpose

Before we explore our individual giftings in further detail, it is important to first distinguish the gifts of God's Spirit from our innate personalities. After all, our personalities are a gift to us from God as well. God created us in his image (see Genesis 1:26–27).

In Psalm 139:13–14, we read that we are "fearfully and wonderfully made." God formed our inward parts, "knitting" us together in our mother's womb. This is a wonderful picture of the personal craftsmanship of God. He is precise in forming each person. From our birth, God has created us for a specific and unique function in his mission in the world.

The gifting that Paul describes in 1 Corinthians 12:1–11 and Romans 12:5–8 refers to more than just this hardwiring we are given at birth. These are gift from God's Spirit, meaning they come to us when we become Christians. These gifts may build on our innate personalities, but they add something unique to who we are—and they are for a divine purpose.

An illustration of this type of gifting from God's Spirit is found in a story from the Old Testament. The Israelites had been set free from bondage in Egypt and were camping in the wilderness on their way to the Promised Land. There, in the desert, the Lord instructed his people (through Moses) to construct a temporary place where the Israelites could worship him, known as the "tabernacle" or "tent of meeting." As the narrative unfolds, we see God clearly endowing people in the community with specific gifts to serve his divine purposes:

> [1] Then the LORD said to Moses, [2] "See, I have chosen Bezalel son of Uri, the son of Hur, of the tribe of Judah, [3] and I have filled him with the Spirit of God, with wisdom, with understanding, with knowledge and with all kinds of skills—[4] to make artistic designs for work in gold, silver and bronze, [5] to cut and set stones, to work in wood, and to engage in all kinds of crafts. [6] Moreover, I have appointed Oholiab son of Ahisamak, of the tribe of Dan, to help him. Also I have given ability to all the skilled workers to make everything I have commanded you: [7] the tent of meeting, the ark of the covenant law with the atonement cover on it, and all the other furnishings of the tent— [8] the table and its articles, the pure gold lampstand and all its accessories, the altar of incense, [9] the altar of burnt offering and all its utensils, the basin with its stand—[10] and also the woven garments, both the sacred garments for Aaron the priest and the garments for his sons when they serve as priests, [11] and the anointing oil and fragrant incense for the Holy Place. They are to make them just as I commanded you."
>
> Exodus 31:1-11

Bezalel was handpicked by God, filled with his Spirit, and uniquely gifted in craftsmanship and artistic design. These talents were not random but were bestowed by the Lord for a specific mission—to contribute to the construction of the tabernacle. Later, God would bestow his gifts on Deborah, a prophetess and judge mentioned in Judges. Deborah was a charismatic leader, an astute counselor, and a bold military strategist. Her leadership and discernment were not limited by societal norms, which challenged conventional gender roles. Deborah's narrative showcases that God's gifts transcend societal expectations and are tailored to individuals, irrespective of gender, to fulfill his grand design for the salvation narrative.

Throughout the Old Testament, this recurring theme of God deliberately granting his gifts underscores the divine intention behind every bestowed gift. These gifts span a spectrum from artistic talents and leadership abilities to prophetic insights and strategic prowess. Whether guiding the construction of sacred structures or leading a nation through challenging times, God's gifts serve as a testament to his inclusive and purposeful plan for humanity.

5. How do the divine appointments of individuals such as Bezalel and Deborah show the diversity of giftings that God gives to people?

6. Are there certain gifts that you feel are underutilized in the church today? If so, which particular gifts are they—and why do you feel that way?

Take Inventory

Perhaps you are now saying to yourself, *All of this sounds great, but how can I know which gifts God has given me to serve the body of Christ?* There is certainly no shortage of tests or tools that can aid you in discerning which gifts of the Holy Spirit you may possess. But while these tools can be helpful, there are other simple ways you can take inventory in your own life.

First, consider where you have seen evidence of joy in your service. What makes you come alive? Maybe it comes from declaring the Word of God in front of a group. Or maybe you come alive when you help to organize a big event or community mission project. It is often the case that people find joy when they are doing something they love and something that they know they are good at doing. Just as a gifted golfer is likely to find much joy on the golf course, so Christians will find much joy in the areas where they are most gifted to serve.

Another clue as to how God has gifted you is to look for areas in which you've had success or seen evidence of God's blessing. Notice any ways you have served that have proven fruitful to others. For instance, if you are gifted in leadership, you may be able to recall situations in which your leadership made others better. If you are gifted in mercy, you likely have a long list of people who have been encouraged and blessed by your ministry in a time of need. This doesn't mean that you have *always* had success in these areas. Even the aforementioned golfer will make an errant shot here or there. But it does mean that the general trajectory is one of effectiveness and skill. The same is true in the church—God's people should take notice of those areas where they have proven effective.

A final clue to knowing your gifts is to consider the feedback of others. What gifts do people point out in your life? This is yet another reason why it is so important to have close relationships with those in the church, as the people who know you the best will be able to point out things about you that you might not be able to see. This will be particularly true at the outset of your spiritual journey. You might be a bit insecure to serve or lack the insight to know how to step in and make a difference. You need people around you who can encourage you to take a risk and help you to discern what you are doing well and what you need to avoid.

Without the help of others, we are all prone to miss clear evidences of God's grace in our lives. We are also likely to miss out on opportunities to be faithful in using the gifts that God has bestowed on us in this day and time. As the disciple Peter pointed out:

7 The end of all things is near. Therefore be alert and of sober mind so that you may pray. 8 Above all, love each other deeply, because love covers over a multitude of sins. 9 Offer hospitality to one another without grumbling. 10 Each of you should use whatever gift you have received to serve others, as faithful stewards of God's grace in its various forms. 11 If anyone speaks, they should do so as one who speaks the very words of God. If anyone serves, they should do so with the strength God provides, so that in all things God may be praised through Jesus Christ. To him be the glory and the power for ever and ever. Amen.

1 Peter 4:7–11

7. Where do you find the most joy in serving? What are some areas in which you have been especially effective in your service to the church?

8. What gifts have other people called out in your life? (If you don't know, reach out to a few people and write their answers in the space below.)

REFLECT

What is often lost in conversations on spiritual gifts is the overall aim. The point is not simply to understand your gifts so that you can feel important or useful in the church. In fact, your gifts aren't actually about you at all. No, we are after a more important goal. As Paul wrote in Ephesians 4:11–16, God gave to his church leaders who are called to equip the saints for the work of the ministry so that the church can be built up. This establishes a key pattern: *Leaders equip all of God's people so that all of God's people can build up all of God's people.*

This sentence may seem redundant, but the refrain is important. It's not merely that leaders build up God's people, and it's not that some of God's people build up the rest of the church. Rather, it's that *all* of God's people build up *all* of God's people. We each exist for the sake of the whole. The image of the church as a body is again helpful at this point. God put his church together in such a way that all parts play different roles within the overall whole. Some are "hands." Some are "legs." Some are "eyes." Together, they work to make the entire body function. Again, if you take one part away, the entire body suffers.

You might not think this is true when it comes to the local church, particularly if you attend a large church filled with talented people. Your assumption might be that your presence and gifts don't matter all that much—that if you don't show up and use your gifts, then surely someone else will. But such a posture minimizes the work of God in building his church. Your presence among the people of God is no accident. Of course, there may be dozens of "thumbs" or "ankles" in the body, but there is no one exactly like you who has been embedded in the same relational structure as you are. Even large churches need dozens of body parts existing in multiple places to build up their members in love and good deeds. You have been placed by a sovereign God in his church to play a unique role among the people he has given you.

This means that you have to show up. Your ongoing presence among the people of God matters, because without you the church will suffer. Those who need your compassion will be neglected. Those who need to learn from your wisdom will miss out. This also means that you have to apply yourself. You can't merely saunter into a service, sit in the back, and slouch there in apathy. The church needs you to give your best—by actively using the gifts that God has provided to you—because the faith of others depends on you using those gifts.

9. What is the role of leaders in the church when it comes to equipping its members for ministry? What is then the role of the individual members in the church?

10. In what ways are you currently showing up and applying yourself in the church? What are some ways that you could lean in a bit more?

CLOSE

As you wrap up this study, think about the role that God has called you to play in his mission. Remember, the church is at the very center of the mission of God. Everything the church does is meant to be on mission. Every person in the church is uniquely gifted by God to play a part in that mission. As people made in God's image and fashioned by his hand, we each play a specific role in emphasizing the mission of God to the ends of the earth.

May God hasten the day when the earth is filled with the knowledge of the glory of God as the waters cover the sea (see Habakkuk 2:14). For this to happen, each person must live on mission through the local church and see to it that their circle of influence is filled with the knowledge of the glory of God. Our neighbors. Our co-workers. Our family members. The people in our world. They all need to see and hear the good news of Jesus Christ. But there's more. They also need to see and hear the good news of Jesus Christ *through us*.

11. As you consider everything you've learned in this study, how would you summarize the way you contribute to the work of your local church?

12. How has God wired you to build the church up in love and good deeds? How might your past have shaped the ways you are now equipped to serve others?

NEXT

In these six lessons of *Church,* we have seen how God purposefully gave his followers a vital mission after Jesus' resurrection and ascension into heaven. We have seen how these followers experienced the power of the Holy Spirit, began to gather into communities to serve one another, and shared with those who were in need. We learned a bit about the persecution they suffered, which caused them to scatter . . . taking the good news of Jesus wherever they went. We also saw how God gathered both Jews and Gentiles into a new family of brothers and sisters in Christ and how all believers—both back then and today—are called to use their gifts for others.

In *Forever,* the next and final study in this series, we will take a look at the end of God's story. We will see that at a time only the Father knows, everything in heaven and on earth will be put right once and for all. Those who are opposed to Jesus will get what they have asked for—an eternity without the Lord's goodness and glory. Conversely, we will also see how those who are redeemed in Christ will gather in his presence from every race and nation, singing the song of Jesus who rescued them from death and brought them into unending life.

Thank you for taking this journey! Stay the course. God has a lot that he wants to do in your life!

Note

1. James D. Bratt, editor, *Abraham Kuyper: A Centennial Reader* (Grand Rapids, MI: William B. Eerdmans, 1998), 488.

LEADER'S GUIDE

Thank you for your willingness to lead your group through this study. What you have chosen to do is valuable and will make a great difference in the lives of others. The rewards of being a leader are different from those of participating, and we hope that as you lead, you will find your own walk with Jesus deepened by the experience.

The lessons in this study guide are suitable for church classes, Bible studies, and small groups. Each lesson is structured to provoke thought and help you grow in your knowledge and understanding of Christ. There are multiple components in this section that can help you structure your lessons and discussion time, so make sure you read and consider each one.

BEFORE YOU BEGIN

Before your first meeting, make sure the group members have a copy of this study guide so they can follow along and have their answers written out ahead of time. Alternately, you can hand out the study guides at your first meeting and give the group members some time to look over the material and ask any preliminary questions. During your first meeting, be sure to send a sheet of paper around the room and have the members write down their name, phone number, and email address so you can keep in touch with them during the week.

Generally, the ideal size for a group is eight to ten people, which will ensure that everyone has enough time to participate in discussions. If you have more people, you might want to break up the main group into smaller subgroups. Encourage those who show up at the first meeting to commit to attending for the duration of the study. This will help the group members get to know one another, create stability for the group, and help you, as the leader, know how to best prepare each week.

Try to initiate a free-flowing discussion as you go through each lesson. Invite group members to bring any questions they have or insights they discover as they go through the content to the next meeting, especially if they were unsure of the meaning of some parts of the lesson. Be prepared to discuss the biblical truth that relates to each topic in the study.

WEEKLY PREPARATION

As the group leader, here are a few things you can do to prepare for each meeting:

- Make sure you understand the content of the lesson so you know how to structure group time and are prepared to lead group discussion.
- Depending on how much time you have each week, you may not be able to reflect on every question. Select specific questions that you feel will evoke the best discussion.
- At the end of your discussion, take prayer requests from your group members and pray for each other.

STRUCTURING THE DISCUSSION TIME

It is up to you to keep track of the time and keep things on schedule. You might want to set a timer for each question that you discuss so both you and the group members know when your time is up. (There are some good phone apps for timers that play a gentle chime or other pleasant sound instead of a disruptive noise.)

Don't be concerned if the group members are quiet or slow to share. People are often quiet when they are pulling together their ideas, and this might be a new experience for them. Just ask a question and let it hang in the air until someone shares. You can then say, "Thank you. What about others? What thoughts came to you?"

If you need help in organizing your time when planning your group Bible study, the following schedule, for sixty minutes and ninety minutes, can give you a structure for the lesson:

	60 Minutes	90 Minutes
Welcome: Arrive and get settled	5 minutes	10 minutes
Message: Review the lesson	15 minutes	25 minutes
Discussion: Discuss study questions	35 minutes	45 minutes
Prayer: Pray together and dismiss	5 minutes	10 minutes

GROUP DYNAMICS

Leading a group through *Church* will prove to be highly rewarding both to you and your group members. But you still may encounter challenges along the way! Discussions can get off track. Group members may not be sensitive to the needs and ideas of others. Some might worry they will be expected to talk about matters that make them feel awkward. Others may express comments that result in disagreements. To help ease this strain on you and the group, consider the following ground rules:

- When someone raises a question or comment that is off the main topic, suggest that you deal with it at another time, or, if you feel led to go in that direction, let the group know you will be spending some time discussing it.

- If someone asks a question that you don't know how to answer, admit it and move on. At your discretion, feel free to invite group members to comment on questions that call for personal experience.

- If you find one or two people are dominating the discussion time, direct a few questions to others in the group. Outside the main group time, ask the more dominating members to help you draw out the quieter ones. Work to make them a part of the solution instead of the problem.

- When a disagreement occurs, encourage the group members to process the matter in love. Encourage those on opposite sides to restate what they heard the other side say about the matter, and then invite each side to evaluate if that perception is accurate. Lead the group in examining other scriptures related to the topic and look for common ground.

When any of these issues arise, encourage your group members to follow these words from the Bible: "Love one another" (John 13:34); "If it is possible, as far as it depends on you, live at peace with everyone" (Romans 12:18); "Whatever is true . . . noble . . . right . . . if anything is excellent or praiseworthy—think about such things" (Philippians 4:8); and "Be quick to listen, slow to speak and slow to become angry" (James 1:19). This will make your group time more rewarding and beneficial for everyone who attends.

Thank you again for your willingness to lead your group. May God reward your efforts and dedication, equip you to guide your group in the weeks ahead, and make your time together fruitful for his kingdom.

ABOUT THE AUTHORS

Aaron Coe has spent more than twenty years working in the non-profit and philanthropic space. Much of that time was spent in New York City in the years after 9/11, helping with revitalization efforts. Aaron served as vice president at North American Mission Board, providing strategic guidance and leadership. He has also worked with organizations like Passion, illumiNations, Food for the Hungry, the Ethics and Religious Liberty Commission, and many others. Aaron has a Ph.D. in Applied Theology and teaches at Dallas Theological Seminary. He is the founder of Future City Now, which seeks to help visionary leaders maximize their influence in the world. Additionally, Aaron served as the General Editor of *The Jesus Bible*. Aaron lives in Atlanta with his wife, Carmen, and their four children.

Matthew Rogers holds a Ph.D. in Applied Theology and teaches and writes on Christian mission, ministry, and discipleship. Notably, Matthew served as the lead writer for the bestselling *The Jesus Bible*. He and his wife, Sarah, and their five children live in Greenville, South Carolina, where Matthew serves as the pastor of Christ Fellowship Cherrydale.

The Jesus Bible Study Series

Beginnings
ISBN 9780310154983

Revolt
ISBN 9780310155003

People
ISBN 9780310155027

Savior
ISBN 9780310155041

Church
ISBN 9780310155065

Forever
ISBN 9780310155089
On sale September 2024

Available wherever books are sold

The Jesus Bible

sixty-six books. one story. all about one name.

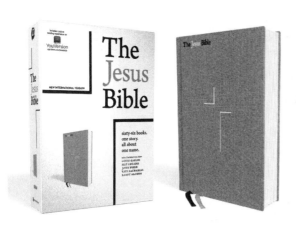

The Jesus Bible, NIV & ESV editions, with feature essays from Louie Giglio, Max Lucado, John Piper, and Randy Alcorn, as well as profound yet accessible study features will help you meet Jesus throughout Scripture.

- 350 full page articles
- 700 side-bar articles
- Book introductions
- Room for journaling

The Jesus Bible Journal, NIV
Study individual books of the Bible featuring lined journal space and commentary from *The Jesus Bible.*

- 14 journals covering 30 books of the Bible
- 2 boxed sets (OT & NT)

TheJesusBible.com

Video Study for Your Church or Small Group

In this six-session video Bible study, bestselling author and pastor Louie Giglio helps you apply the principles in *Don't Give the Enemy a Seat at Your Table* to your life. The study guide includes access to six streaming video sessions, video notes and a comprehensive structure for group discussion time, and personal study for deeper reflection between sessions.

Study Guide + Streaming Video
9780310156284

DVD
9780310134268

Available now at your favorite bookstore
or streaming video on StudyGateway.com.

 passionpublishing

 Harper*Christian* Resources